MARRIAGE UNCUT III

Straight Talk, No Chaser
An Anthology

PROSPERING IN A PANDEMIC

Tenita C. Johnson

Published by So It Is Written, LLC
Detroit, MI
SoItIsWritten.net

Marriage Uncut III: Straight Talk, No Chaser, Prospering in a Pandemic
Copyright © 2020 by Tenita C. Johnson

All rights reserved. No part of this book may be reproduced or transmitted in any form or by any means, electronic or mechanical, including photocopying, recording, or by an information storage and retrieval system - except by a reviewer who may quote brief passages in a review to be printed in a magazine or newspaper - without permission in writing from the publisher.

Edit by: So It Is Written – www.SoItIsWritten.net

Formatting: Ya Ya Ya Creative – www.yayayacreative.com

ISBN No. 978-1-7346602-6-5

LCCN: 2020915643

PRINTED AND BOUND IN THE UNITED STATES OF AMERICA

OTHER WORKS
by Tenita C. Johnson

100 Words of Encouragement:
Tidbits of Inspiration

100 Words of Encouragement:
Tidbits of Inspiration – Audio Book

100 Words of Encouragement II: Driven to Dream

When the Smoke Clears: A Phoenix Rises

Grammatically Incorrect:
When Commas Save Your Sentences & Your Reputation

From Fatherless To Fearless

The Wait of Success:
How to Become an Overnight Success in 7,300 Days

Marriage Uncut: Straight Talk, No Chaser

Marriage Uncut II: Straight Talk, No Chaser

How to Write a Bestselling Memoir

How to Write a 30-Day Devotional in 48 Hours

Available at SoItIsWritten.net and Amazon.com

Table of Contents

Foreword 1
   About the Author: LaShun Franklin, MA & LLP 5

Beauty & The Beast 9
   About the Author: K. V. Banks 27

The Notebook 31
   About the Author: Tiffany Banks 47

Mr. & Mrs. Smith: Let Me Reintroduce Myself .. 51
   About the Author: Ray Shipman 67

Endless Love 71
   About the Author: Nakeya Shipman 87

Love & Basketball 91
   About the Author: Celeste Blackman 105

Do the Right Thing 111
   About the Author: Ortavia McClain 125

Brown Sugar 129
   About the Author: Tenita C. Johnson 139

About: So It Is Written 141

About: The Red Ink Conference 143

Foreword
by LaShun Franklin, MA, LLP

Marriage. The oldest and first relationship designed in the earth, as we know it. The very foundation of most societies exist because a man and a woman made a choice (or it was chosen for them) to be in a committed relationship. In Western culture, we have many catch phrases that try to describe the journey of marriage. While some are positive, others are negative. However, what it all boils down to is this: *marriage is hard work!*

Many married couples spent more time dreaming about their lives together and planning a wedding than they did preparing for the new job description of husband or wife. Many of us had to figure it out as we went along, evaluating daily if the investment was even worth it! Many of our predecessors hid the work and presented to us a scripted look at marriage, which unfortunately could have never properly prepared us for what came next.

In Matthew 19:11-12, in the Message translation, Jesus has some "real talk" with the Pharisees and His disciples: *But Jesus said, "Not everyone is mature enough to live a married life. It requires a certain aptitude and grace. Marriage isn't for everyone. Some, from birth seemingly, never give marriage a thought. Others never get asked - or accepted. And some decide not to get married for kingdom reasons. But if you're capable of growing into the largeness of marriage, do it."*

Jesus clarifies a couple of things that people need to understand well *before* they enter a marriage. In verse 11, the key is that not everyone is *mature* enough to live a married life. In verse 12, He reiterates his message saying, "Marriage will *grow you up, if you're up to the challenge!*" This is not a negative statement; however, it is a very encouraging one. Jesus is encouraging us to examine our own capacity to love others and please God in doing so. The earlier verses in this 19th chapter support God's original plan for marriage and what standard He is expecting from those of us who choose marriage.

Marriage Uncut III: Straight Talk, No Chaser, Prospering in a Pandemic is an "in your face" look at the real work of real marriages. It gives us a very raw and uncut look at the potential situations that every marriage may experience and the decisions that the writers chose when faced with these challenges. Reading this book feels like you are interviewing a couple on a scripted reality television show. Some situations may echo your own, or may mirror the lives of someone you know. You may find yourself laughing, crying or praying with and for these couples as they share their candid truths. The level of transparency may even feel slightly embarrassing, at times, but you will 'get it'! We get to witness the *maturation* and *expansion* opportunities that marriage offers, in the wake of personality differences, mistakes, trials and lack of knowledge.

Unfortunately, we do not currently live in a culture or nation that supports healthy marriage, like it did in earlier years. With a 50-60% divorce rate in the U.S., and the decline of the traditional family, we have to take a hard look at how we can help others make good, healthy decisions concerning marriage. In the many years of providing counsel and mentoring for couples, I have found that good preparation, tools, support and transparency is key to helping couples thrive. In the event that challenges occur during marriage (which they will), having transparent, mature mentors and accountability is golden! This anthology is not for the person who chooses to hide behind the face of religion or fantasy. The uncut nature of their accounts can be used as a teaching tool to provide readers with hope, insight and courage to make better choices in their own marriage.

I leave you with my life's motto: "Marriage is good. Family is good. Marriage is work, and it is a good work. Everything can be fixed, so let us get on with it!"

About the Author
➥ LaShun Franklin, MA & LLP

While many people choose to brush their issues under the rug, LaShun Franklin, MA & LLP, removes the rug altogether, helping clients deal with their issues head on. Realizing that it's often easier for people to hide behind the masks of guilt, shame and error, Franklin works wholeheartedly to usher her clientele into their purpose, passion and prosperity. Specializing in mood disorders, anxiety, ADHD, and grief, she teaches her clients that in order to effectively live, one must die to self on a daily basis.

In addition to holding a Bachelor of Science in Psychology and a Master of Arts in Marriage and Family Therapy, she is also certified as a Limited Licensed Psychologist by the State of Michigan and a Trauma and Loss Specialist. Her tenacity to help clients heal from past wounds, coupled with her educational background, opened doors for her to lead Facilitating Open Couple Communication, Understanding and Study (F.O.C.C.U.S.) and the Prevention and Relationship Enhancement Program (P.R.E.P.). Obtaining ministerial training from Rhema Bible

College, certification from Light University, and her license through Destiny Outreach Ministerial Alliance (DOMA), Franklin has made it her mission to restore broken marriages and families—one client at a time.

Serving as a master-level psychotherapist, she uses a wide variety of theory-based techniques, such as Cognitive Behavioral, Rational Emotive Therapy, Solution-focused Brief Techniques, Play-based Activities and Gestalt Psychology. Through her creative strategy efforts and out-of-the-box problem-solving techniques, Franklin helps her clients realize that success truly happens—not when you have all of the answers to life's questions—but when you are able to face the questions you've been avoiding your whole life.

Understanding that life is often driven by relationships, she coaches couples, families and individuals alike on how to set boundaries, sever ties with unhealthy relationships, rebuild self-esteem and live the abundant life the way God intended. As a master motivator, teacher and purpose coach, she is committed to helping her clients turn their worry and wounds into wisdom. And while many will tell you that time heals all wounds, she will argue that healing—true healing—only comes to those who are willing to peel back the layers and do the work.

For appointments or more information, please email lashun@songsofsolomonri.com or call 313-794-5152.

Beauty & The Beast
by K. V. Banks

Saturday, July 20, 2019. The day I had been anticipating for a long time. In fact, it was a day I felt would never come for me. It was the day I was joined in holy matrimony to God's greatest creation: my beautiful wife, Tiffany. The level of excitement I felt thinking about how great life was going to be married to the love of my life was immeasurable. But it wasn't until we entered the marriage that I learned that my own personal perceptions, expectations and mentality of what a marriage is supposed to look like would make for a rocky start.

Some wise friends told me that all the advice in the world couldn't properly prepare me for marriage. Some things I would just learn once I said, "I do!" One friend even said, "No one can truly prepare you for marriage because none of us have ever been married to Tiffany." As there are general characteristics of women overall, every married man I spoke with could only give me advice from their personal experiences. And those experiences have been specific to their lives with their own wives. So, I would have to learn what life was like to be married to my Tiffany.

So, let's take a look at some of the things that formed my perspective of married life and even a deeper look at the things that forged my insecurities.

A Picture of True Love

My first example of a godly marriage came from my spiritual parents, Pastor David and Lady Gayle Fielder. I've heard their love story so many times that I could recite it back almost verbatim, even down to the dates. To have met hundreds of miles away from home at a national convention, only to find out that not only were they from the same city, but they lived less than seven minutes apart from each other, was nothing short of amazing. Growing up in my home church, I paid close attention to those small things. I paid attention to how they talked about each other and, more specifically, how she treated him. I've seen couples who seemed to be off balance (from my perspective). One would praise the other and they seemed to be so in love, but the other never gave the same public display of affection. I noticed how Lady Fielder melted whenever her husband called her name. From my angle, sitting on the organ at church, I could see her staring at him while he preached. Every now and then, I saw a dreamy haze over her eyes accompanied by a huge smile. It was almost like a movie where you could see birds flying around her head. With thirty plus years of marriage, that's something to take note of!

Pastor Fielder has never been shy about sharing his love for his wife. Anyone who doesn't know that they are in love, obviously hasn't met them before. He's a huge family man! He believes in taking care of his home and making sure every need in his house is met. These are things that he taught me growing up, which I still hold on to this day. However, he has a dominate personality with a huge presence, which commands a room in seconds. I believe it's largely due to his background as a police officer and even growing up as a football player. For years, I admired the relationship they had. It felt like if I was going to have a happy marriage like theirs, I had to be the same type of man he is, as opposed to just being who I am.

As our wedding date approached, I felt an enormous amount of pressure. I was beyond stressed out. I was actually glad I decided to go bald several years ago because my hair probably would've fallen out on its own while preparing for that wedding. It wasn't just because of the stress that comes with planning a wedding. It was the stress of believing that I had to conform into this image of what I needed to be as a husband, which I felt I wasn't fit for quite yet. Part of me was excited and I believed I was ready to be married. Yet, another part of me felt like I was inadequate, and I wasn't ready to be a husband. However, I had made a resolve that, once we got married, everything would be better. Life would smooth out. Yeah…it didn't *quite* happen that way.

I Saw That Going Differently

Once we were wed, I expected an instant change. Like a fairytale where they sprinkle dust on you and you become a different person, I expected something magical to happen. To an extent, for me, I did. I felt like the full weight of our marriage was on my shoulders. If something was going to be done, I had to do it. Problem was, I was struggling. I wasn't communicating that struggle to my wife, though. I felt like it would make me less of a man if I wasn't able to pay the full amount of the rent, or if I wasn't able to give anything toward the bills at all. In those first several months, I felt like a failure. It's crazy because I honestly felt like I was being emasculated because of the financial structure of our home.

My wife is a full-time employee at Wayne State University, with a remarkably high position as a business manager. I said I wasn't intimidated by it. But, deep down, I was a little bit insecure. *How am I supposed to be the breadwinner when she's making the type of money she is? I'm a full-time entrepreneur who's building a music school after losing his job as a radio production engineer two months before his wedding* (and now you see where the added stress came from). During 2019, my music school struggled harder than it ever did since its inception in 2016. In fact, when we returned from our honeymoon, my student enrollment was down to five. *How am I supposed to pay any bills with only five students!* I thought. I was struggling and trying to find money anywhere I could get it. I had been driving for Uber for a while, trying to make ends meet before. So, I just drove even more for Uber. In fact, I was Uber-ing the day before my wedding.

All of this happened because I *wouldn't*—not I *couldn't*—talk to my wife and tell her what was going on. I felt I was responsible for making everything happen financially, not knowing she was already working in the background and making things happen. She had things set aside to cover me if I needed it. As grateful as I was for her doing it, it just wasn't what I convinced myself of how things would be for us. I saw myself carrying the full financial load and her money going toward small things. Maybe she would just put it away in savings altogether. I thought that was how a man is supposed to run his home. But it took a while to learn that leading your home doesn't mean killing yourself to do everything yourself. In all of this, I was ignoring the biggest element in our marriage: *teamwork*. We were a *team*. We had been a team before, and we would be a team afterward. When I came to grips with that reality, I saw a big difference in our home.

It took a while for me to finally open up and start talking about what was going on and start putting a plan together on how to make things happen for our home. I've always been told that the biggest key in marriage is communication. So, I tried to start communicating with my wife, but I found that things didn't always go as planned. Even trying to talk about certain things would be misinterpreted or misunderstood. That's because I wanted her to receive information the way

I received it. That's when I learned that the biggest key to a marriage isn't communication—it's *comprehension*. You can believe you're communicating with an individual, but if they aren't comprehending what you're saying, it's all for naught. When I started accepting the fact that my wife wasn't looking for me to be perfect but just upfront and honest, it opened a huge door for us to speak freely and work together as a team.

Beauty and the Beast

For years, I struggled with my weight. Over the years, I vacillated up and down in my weight. Throughout school, I developed a terrible self-image and even fortified a huge insecurity. I believed I would never obtain true happiness in a relationship. I felt like the woman I desired to be with would never want to be with someone who looked like me. It caused me to settle into relationships with anyone who showed any inkling of acceptance toward me. Yet, God sent a woman who honestly looks like the picture I had seen for years, but never felt I was worthy enough to share the frame with.

When we started dating, I was at my biggest weight: over 350 pounds. Before we started dating and we were just friends, I learned that she had a certain type of man that she liked. Her track record proved it. All of them had a similar type of build that looked nothing like me.

So, when we started dating, I felt like I needed to lose weight, or I feared losing her. She never said this to me, nor did she insinuate the thought that her faithfulness to me was contingent upon my ability to lose weight. But this was the reality I fostered in my head. I lived in that reality for years.

We often went downtown to exercise by walking and jogging along the Detroit Riverwalk. We would even walk up and down the steps of the old Joe Louis Arena. I felt like I needed to do this to prove to her that I wanted to lose the weight. I would do whatever I had to do to be with her. She showed me over and over again that she loved me *for me*.

But I still wanted to give her what I believed she wanted. In my mind, I still needed to do this to gain her acceptance.

This insecurity had been in existence longer than I'd even known her. She was trying to show me what the true love of God looked like. Yet, my eyes were clouded by what the enemy made me believe was the truth: you will never be happy in the state you're in, and you'll lose her to someone else if you don't change.

As the years went on, the power of her love toward me demolished the wall of insecurity. I changed the way I looked at myself. I worked out more—not because I wanted her acceptance—but simply because I wanted to be healthier. My wall was crumbling, but it wasn't completely gone. The final blow to this wall wouldn't come until after we said, "I do."

Because of years of dealing with a poor self-image, low self-esteem and even depression, I destroyed myself internally. As a preacher and public figure, I'm very cognizant of how I'm perceived outwardly. As a preacher, I know how to speak words of encouragement and uplift others, while I'm going through my own storm behind closed doors. I really needed the very words I was giving to others. As a comedian, I know how to make everyone else laugh and have a good time while, inwardly, I had been crying, wishing I could have the same joy everyone else was experiencing. As an actor, I know how to create an entirely different façade, which makes people think my reality is completely different from what I'm truly dealing with in real life.

With that, the enemy gave me the gift of porn and the timeline of life destruction began. I can't say I was addicted to porn; I honestly fell in love with it. I was infatuated with it. It became the only place I could escape to, where I engulfed myself and felt accepted. The main lie the enemy told me was, "When you get married, you won't need this anymore. You'll have a wife!" I believed him. But little did I know, porn was setting me up for failure! For years, I learned patterns and habits that weren't even realistic.

The accessibility of porn hardwires the mindset that, whenever you're ready, you can have it. Day or night. Sunshine or rain, it doesn't matter. If you are in the mood (which, for men, tends to be a little bit more than women), it's available for you. Well, I later learned that it doesn't honestly work like that in marriage. Because I equated porn with acceptance, when my wife wasn't in the mood, or when she just wasn't able to be with me in that way, I saw her rejecting the act as rejecting me. However, I later realized that porn was setting me up for bigger issues.

Due to the fact that I'd spent years of my life indulging in pornography, I constructed an image of what those intimate moments should be like in my marriage. Without realizing it, I was robbing my wife of the ability to just be who she is because I placed my unrealistic expectations on her. In essence, porn made it increasingly difficult to connect with my wife and appreciate her for her. I wanted her to be like what I'd become accustomed to. I wanted her to be like what I was used to seeing since I was fifteen years old.

When the revelation came that porn was actually destroying my intimate life and was, in fact, creating a hindrance to the closeness I longed to have with my wife, I fervently sought God for help. I sought Him once and for all to set me free from this unremitting cycle. Even though I'd prayed this prayer before, this time was different. For the first time, I saw how my addiction was affecting someone else who I deeply loved. It wasn't just about me anymore. Now, I was placing false expectations and unnecessary pressure on my wife to be someone she could never be. I didn't want this for her. I wanted my wife to be enough. I wanted to be satisfied with her and her alone.

As time went on, I saw an interesting turn of events. I noticed how increasingly beautiful my wife was becoming. My wife has always been beautiful to me, but it seemed as if her beauty was intensifying. I felt like I'd went to the eye doctor and picked up new frames with a new prescription. Before you go to the eye doctor, you feel like you can see simply fine. But once you get in the chair and they change your prescription in the lenses, you see with added clarity. Without the cloud of porn and false expectations, I was finally able to take in the awesomeness of what I've had in front of me all along.

The greatest part about this newfound infatuation with my wife is that it wasn't *all* sexually motivated. The attraction I felt wasn't because I was trying to "get it on." I saw how beautiful she was all around, not just physically. I saw her drive for ministry, her love for life, her dedication to school, and her attentiveness to me. I saw all she was juggling, and she was killing it on every front! These are things that my clouded mind couldn't see before.

Here Comes COVID-19

COVID-19 came at an interesting time. It caused a lot of uncertainty and fear. Not knowing what would happen from week to week was not comfortable. We saw people we knew and loved infected by the virus and some, unfortunately, lost their battles. It was a daily fight for us to remain positive in the process. However, one thing the pandemic created for us was a lot of time together. During that time, we were able to create a new normal. But it wasn't easy. It was rough seeing the toll this virus took on our nation and even our home. I fought hard to maintain the image of strength and confidence before my wife, while ignoring the unshakable fear I felt on the inside. But in this, we were able to deal with the issues that we'd avoided for too long. At the same time, it allowed us to experience a side of our marriage that we'd never known.

What happens when a quiet, corporate executive and college student, and a noisy music teacher have to work within the same space? You get tension and some tough workdays! She's used to peace and quiet, and I like noise. Even when I'm trying to concentrate, I need some noise. I like music in the background if I'm not the one making it myself.

When I was in my music studio, I was loud with my students. We played games, made music and had fun. That's the environment I was used to. I'm an extrovert. I like talking and laughing. So, trying to recreate that same workspace proved to be a bit of a challenge. My wife doesn't work in that type of environment. She works in the corporate world. She does well sitting at a desk and knocking out work. I've worked a corporate job before, and I made it out, only by the grace of God. *I could not stand it.* It was the opposite of what I wanted to do. I wanted to have fun and make noise. Instead, I had to be quiet and work. It was torture. Being able to create my own work environment is a luxury I pray I never have to go without again!

However, the quarantine showed me how much time apart we really spent away from each other. Often, by the time I'd make it home, I was tired and ready to be quiet. But now, I was in the house, all day, every day, ready to make noise. But I couldn't do it like I wanted to. *How were we going to make this work in our small apartment?*

When we rented our apartment, we didn't take into consideration that we would both need to work from home. I never saw any reason for me to teach piano from home. Nor did she foresee having to work off campus. But here we are, with two different careers, and two different paths, colliding into one small space. This is where we learned the art of *compromise*. We tried it several different ways and with multiple arrangements. We were finally able to find a medium that works for us. We hit a point where I'm learning to work with her deadening quietness, and she's learning to manage my noise. The great thing about it is that we remain considerate of each other in order to make it work. I know she understands that my job requires me to make some noise, but I try not to overdo it. I learned how to become *selfless*.

Outside of the trials of having to work in the same space together, I was also concerned about our family's income. As I mentioned before, when we first got married, I only had five students. Through the favor and grace of God, we had grown to twenty-five students in just a few short months. Things were looking great, and a door even opened for us to launch into a second location, which would only expand the school even more! But with the impact of COVID, many families unenrolled from classes because they either had been physically affected by the virus, they were facing financial hardships that made every dollar questionable, or they just didn't want to take lessons virtually. Through that, I lost more than ten students in a matter of two weeks. It had taken me several months to make the progress I had. Within just two weeks, I'd lost half of my students!

These are the moments that prove if you are really with the correct mate. Words spoken in critical moments like these speak volume of a person's character. My wife spoke life to me and ensured me that everything was going to be alright. She kept pushing me to keep going and to trust God to navigate us through this. She targeted my fear points and helped push me into my next level. A lot of limits and mental barriers were removed during the quarantine. A lot of things I saw as "beyond me," "above my skillset" or "long-term goals and dreams" became very real, very obtainable and very prevalent in the midst of a famine. I stopped telling myself what I couldn't do, and I focused instead on what I could do. Those words my wife spoke to me encouraged me to move on. It was simply the icing on the cake of what she had been doing all along.

The Power of True Love

It was not until I entered my marriage that I realized how much I was hindering my own progress in life. I made people think I was making it happen. People thought I was making big strides in life. But my own negative view of my own abilities kept me operating on a mediocre level. The worst part about it is that I didn't see it. I just believed that there were certain things I wasn't going to be able to do based off lies the enemy had been telling me for years. But, through the weight of love given to me through our marriage, I have found freedom and joy on a level I never knew existed. Her love acted as a bulldozer, destroying my wall of insecurity.

One of the biggest things the love of my wife did for me was completely change my self-image. I had the "beauty and the beast" syndrome. I felt like that's how we looked when we were together. This woman is absolutely gorgeous. Yet, here I was. I was a bit on the heavier side, not the chiseled guy you'd see on the cover of a magazine. Yet, I managed to be with someone as beautiful as my wife. Her love showed me that I am good enough and I am wanted. I didn't need to lose weight to win over her love and affection. Getting in shape wouldn't keep her around. Me losing weight is simply so I can be healthy and enjoy this new life God has blessed me with.

The words my wife spoke over me didn't just change how I felt about myself physically—but mentally, as well. I stopped putting limitations on myself and stopped self-sabotaging my own progress. I began to think on a new level. My entire perspective changed, along with everything else around me. My music school grew by leaps and bounds because I saw the opportunity in all of this. I was scared and nervous that the shift would hinder my progress, but we have created a new market for ourselves, enrolling students from all over the *nation*. We have had record-breaking months, where we were doubling—and even tripling—our enrollment within just a month's time!

At the top of this pandemic, the Lord spoke a word into my spirit: *"I'm sending growth in the middle of a drought."* That growth applied to many areas of my life. One area I'm grateful for God cultivating is our marriage. I feel a closeness with my wife that I've never felt before. We're freer and I'm excited about the future we have ahead of us. Her love motivates me to give more, to do more and to go further. This pandemic put us through the test and made us evaluate a lot of things. But one thing I know for certain is that, with the right partner, you can make it through any storm.

Marriage Uncut
CHECKPOINT

1. How did the model of marriage presented before you growing up affect you when you first got married?

   _____

   _____

   _____

2. What changes have you made to that model to make it work for your home currently?

   _____

   _____

   _____

3. Have you dealt with pornography in your marriage? Individually or as a couple?

   _____

   _____

   _____

4. What steps did you take (or are you willing to take) to overcome the addiction of porn?

   _____

   _____

   _____

CHECKPOINT, *continued*

5. How does your spouse respond to you when you're in a crisis?

6. What would you like your spouse to say to you to encourage you and motivate you to push forward?

7. How does your spouse comprehend your communication style?

8. How does your spouse receive and process information?

About the Author
➠ K. V. Banks

KiJuan V. Banks, affectionately known to many as K.V., knows firsthand that it doesn't take luck or good fortune to be successful. One must simply be deliberate and intentional about his or her actions and plans. As an entrepreneur, musician, comedian and minister, he's not just on a mission to experience dream and destiny fulfillment himself—but he's committed to creating a new norm and culture for his family, both present and future. He, along with his wife Tiffany, endeavor to create a new legacy of wealth and generational success, as well as exemplify the true love of God through their marriage.

For booking and to stay connected with K.V. Banks, log onto www.KVBanksLive.com.

THE NOTEBOOK
by Tiffany Banks

Having adapted to a fast-paced lifestyle, my husband and I were always on the go. We managed to juggle our brand-new marriage and obligations fairly well. Though we were intentional about the progress of our relationship, I could tell that we were stretched thin in some areas. We collectively perceived that our communication, intimacy and life-building efforts were undoubtedly a work in progress.

Then, COVID-19 hit.

To say the least, this pandemic shook us in unimaginable ways. It has redefined our unit and shifted our focus to areas that would have inevitably been exposed with time.

Thank God! I thought while reflecting on the mental and emotional turmoil we had been experiencing. I was so grateful to have this amazing partner in my life, especially during this time. We've cried together. We've found joy in one another. We can feel one another, sensing when things are weighing heavy on our hearts.

Then, we learned that our communication wasn't so hot.

"How in the world did he get *that* when I clearly said...?" Yeah! We're yet and still navigating through that. I realized how I'd been neglecting him when he needed moral support. I'd become distracted by social media woes, trends and drama. It seems like we're in an accelerated course, learning lessons that may have been years ahead of our time. Because of our will to submit to one another, and to God, the blessings have been overflowing in our life. "Unity" has a new meaning for us now.

COVID-19 rampaged our world, with no formal introduction. It left us speechless and it left us both with feelings of insecurity. Two weeks prior to our state shutting down, we attended our annual jurisdictional workers' meeting, where several attendees had been infected and, sequentially, lost their battle to the coronavirus. We lost so many, so quickly, that it became more and more numbing as the fatalities increased, unfortunately. What was so frightening was that we were in close proximity and vulnerable to being exposed to the virus, as well. What's still surreal is how I felt the urgency to *not* stick around and mingle, as I normally would. Actually, my husband, K.V., recalls a few moments after service when one particular person attempted to speak with him. I circled back a couple of times to grab his hand and escort him out of the sanctuary. We later learned that, indeed, that person had been exposed to the virus, as well. We're convinced that this was God's way of protecting us.

In such uncertain and troubling times, I found safety and comfort in our home and my partner. As a team, we sprang into action, building a regimen to stay healthy (taking immune system builders and vitamins) and we set a shopping schedule. We agreed to make healthier eating choices, to stay hydrated and to keep our heads leveled. Initially, I received resistance about taking the vitamins daily. I shared with my husband that being consistent with this routine was important to me, for numerous reasons. The main one was, quite simply, I just couldn't bear the thought of losing him. From that day forward, he took vitamins daily and did not hesitate to keep me accountable. It felt like we had it all figured out (with the little control we had over the virus). Taking our own precautions, we were also trusting God to keep us.

My sister, who happens to live with my parents, sent me messages to check in (as she did on a daily basis). We were missing our loved ones. She'd kept me updated on my parents' whereabouts and health statuses. She mentioned that my father hadn't been feeling well for several weeks. He was barely eating or getting out of bed, and she didn't know what to do. He was turned away by emergency because he wasn't showing severe-enough symptoms to get tested for COVID-19. My sister had lost her sense of taste and smell, as well. My mother was also under the weather.

All I could do was plead with God to heal my family. I called my father, just wanting to hear his voice. However, I constantly got his voicemail. I later learned that he was really weak and sleeping through the days. After many attempts, I finally got in touch with him.

Hopeful, I asked him, "How are you feeling today?"

"I'm trying to hang in here. Not doing too well." His reply paralyzed me as I stood over the kitchen counter, preparing dinner. Trying to hold back the tears until we ended our call, I told him, "I love you, and everything is going to be okay."

We hung up and I let out a hysterical cry. K.V. darted into the room and wrapped his arms around me, confused.

He asked, "What's wrong?"

Sobbing and attempting to catch my breath, I said, "I don't want my daddy to die!"

He held me tight and began to pray. That night, we reaffirmed our faith. We dismissed the fear and negative thoughts that led me to worry. We became intentional in prayer and shifted our focus back to devotion, creating a new sense of normalcy. Some time passed, and I received a call from my father. He was in good spirits; I could hear the strength in his voice. My mom mentioned that he was eating everything in the house and moving around more. I was so grateful that he finally recovered and that they were all doing much better. Here, I was reminded that I don't always have to be strong. We have good days and rough ones. However, what's certain is that we have one another to lean on. I'm grateful for my husband's praying nature and compassionate heart.

Workspace Chaos Turned Copacetic

Of course, with the stay-at-home order, the new dynamics of our work environment—which was minimized to a one-bedroom apartment—brought about its fair share of challenges. K.V. owns his own music school, and I am a business manager for an academic services division at a university. A normal workday for me is chaotic and fast-paced. A semi-quiet environment is more conducive to a productive day. Need I say more? Mr. Banks is a gentleman. He agreed to teach his classes in our bedroom during the day while I crunched numbers and took conference calls from the living room. We were also running virtual church services from our room on certain weekdays and on the weekends. Later, we decided to move church service to the dining area, which provided more space and better lighting. Needless to say, Mr. Banks got a little taste of something new and made the executive decision to move his music classroom to the dining area (which is about seven feet away from what seemed to be becoming my peacefully quiet workspace).

What's still funny is that he asked me how I felt about the move before he made it. I was against it, and he suggested that I move to the bedroom. *Did I mention that I was against this move?* The resolve? We're office neighbors now. I was definitely annoyed, and I felt like my thoughtful husband was turning into a schmuck. *How inconsiderate! He knows how demanding my job can be!* A few days went by, and the annoyance turned into shame. I thought to myself, *Your husband is trying to run a business. Why do you get to work in a big space, while he's crammed up in a corner? What makes your job more superior to his? His workspace in the dining area definitely looks more professional, and it seems to be a convenient space for him, too.*

Oh, don't worry! The satire beat me into humility. The inconvenience of bringing work home wasn't just impacting me. It had flipped the entire structure of my husband's business upside-down. I put on my big girl pants and made the proper adjustments. For instance, I started taking meetings during his breaks or while he wasn't teaching. I'd put on headphones if his classes were a bit loud. Now, I look forward to being able to look past the arm of our couch just to admire him in his element—and flirt with him from time to time.

FUN FACT: K.V.'s clientele has grown ten times larger *during* this pandemic. Imagine if I continued to be stubborn about a silly workspace and gave him grief about how he could operate his business elsewhere. I would be a hindrance, a burden and an enemy to our home. I'm reminded of Proverbs 14:1, which says, *A wise woman builds her home, but a foolish woman tears it down with her own hands* (NLT). This taught me that giving power to something so insignificant will block the blessings and favor that God has allowed to manifest from the works of your oneness. I was also missing the point: I was blessed to be at home, which is a far better working environment, without interruptions. I was safe, happy, healthy and locked in with my legal best friend *with benefits*.

Imbalance and Neglect

Along with a demanding corporate career, I've recently gone back to school to pursue an MBA. These classes were oddly scheduled and demanded a lot of time for projects, reading and exams. There were days that I'd be so burned out from work and school that I had extraordinarily little to offer my husband. I felt guilty that, most days, I couldn't drag myself into the kitchen and whip him up a good meal. Of course,

I tried! Knowing that my days were full, I'd still map out what I wanted to cook, just to make sure he was taken care of. Before I could think of moving, there he was, cleaning the kitchen and prepping for dinner. It makes my heart smile every time. There were plenty nights that I denied him sex because I could barely keep my eyes open, or I just couldn't get in the mood. As newlyweds, this became too regular and unfair to the both of us. Though K.V. was patient with me, I knew that it was running thin. He had every right to express his frustration with me.

I pondered, "How on earth am I going to balance all of this stuff? I can still have it all, right? I can be a wife, daughter, student, businesswoman, singer and so much more, right? But do I want it all? "I'll take 'most' for $300, Alex!" I chose wisdom rather than filling myself to life's full capacity. Being successful professionally and academically while my marriage, peace and sanity, and health are holding on by a thread just isn't the legacy I desire to perpetuate. On the flipside, I've seized every opportunity I can to step in when I know he's going too hard. I also quickly learned that the nighttime isn't the only *right time* (if you catch my drift).

As a "power couple," it's so easy to get sucked in by the demands of our dreams and aspirations when boundaries aren't set. That's a task in itself, but we're establishing them. This pandemic has shed light on our work ethic and habits.

I admire that we are hard-working professionals and that we diligently work an objective until it's complete. The disadvantages—at times—are the inability to take a breather and recharge, sacrificed sleep and lack of personal time. It has led to mental and physical burnout. I've noticed that, because we're at home, there isn't a structure that forces us to take a lunch break away from the desk. We don't clock out at the end of the day. There's no reminder for us to take a break and walk to stretch our legs. It's so easy to sit in front of a computer all day on a comfy couch or chair, and forget that it's also important to unplug, even for a short moment. I learned this the hard way.

The other challenge was allowing our quality time and free moments to be consumed by social media. It became difficult going so long without interacting with people in person that the primary way to stay connected and up to date with folks was virtually. Some days, I found myself scrolling through Facebook, looking at the same newsfeed habitually out of boredom. After a hard day at work, K.V. would spark a conversation, pouring his heart out about whatever was weighing on him. I realized that I wasn't as attentive as I could have been. He did not have my undivided attention and, sometimes, I didn't have his. In those moments, unfortunately, we missed the opportunity to be present and provide moral support. We lost that time to just be a sounding board for one another. It would be disheartening when he'd bring up a conversation that I was partially listening to and my reaction would further confirm to him that I wasn't listening to anything he was saying. I was disappointing him and, in an indirect way, telling him that his concerns and thoughts weren't important to me. Now, I am more conscientious about being attentive when he wants to share something with me. During our designated quality time, we either put our phones away or place them face-down on the table.

Though I'm aware that communication is always a work in progress, I was under the impression that we were pretty decent communicators. Prior to the pandemic, I don't recall having many miscommunications with my husband. During the pandemic, however, we've had some really wacky moments. Literally, we've put words in each other's mouths. It's still a mystery how it's happened, but we're working to improve how we communicate.

Here's an example. Over pillow talk, I asked my husband what his schedule looked like the next day. He gave me a rundown of what he had planned. He expected to be done in the early afternoon. I mentioned to him that I needed to go grocery shopping for my parents and that I'd like for him to go with me. After shopping for them, I would also need to drop their items off and head straight to a singing engagement on the other side of town (I prefer to get to engagements early to collect myself and prepare to minister). The next day, I did a few things around the house, waiting for him to let me know that he was on his way home. I would make him lunch and we could knock out this grocery run together. So, I thought.

After not hearing from him, I shot him a text, asking what his ETA was.

He replied, "Rehearsal just started."

However, he'd told me he'd be done for the day.

Aimlessly re-reading these three words, this response befuddled me. *What just happened?* Well, after trying to understand what went wrong in our conversation, I fumbled around the house, preparing to make the grocery run alone. By the time I finished shopping, I didn't have time to run the groceries to my parents' home. I was rushing to the other side of town to get to my singing engagement. The venue was in a rough neighborhood, and I had no other choice but to leave the groceries visibly in my car. I prayed that no one would bust my windows out to get them.

"Throw the whole day away!" I said. It was my mantra in that moment.

Communication has always been important to me. This scenario helped me understand that it's okay to over-communicate in order to make sure you and your partner are on the same page. Also, the possible consequences of miscommunication are too large of a price to pay.

Health Challenges

For three straight months, we were locked in our home, only leaving out when our refrigerator was empty and when essentials were running low. It was cold outdoors, so all we wanted to do was stay in our warm and cozy apartment, snuggled under blankets. I recall having aches and pains from not having good back support and sitting for long periods of time. These small aches turned into more noticeable ones. I had poor circulation in my legs and kept developing blood clots. I had a sharp pain shooting through my stomach and back. At first, it was manageable. However, it became progressively worse. I had trouble bending over and lying on my stomach. One day, I felt a knot on my navel. The pain affected my ability to sleep, use the restroom and sit up. It even impacted our moments of intimacy. K.V. took me to urgent care to get it checked out. They couldn't find anything wrong, but it was apparent that something was going terribly wrong. As recommended, I monitored the knot and it shrunk, but the symptoms were periodic. I was finally able to schedule a virtual appointment with my primary care physician (who had just recovered from the coronavirus). Since the appointment was virtual, there wasn't much that my doctor could do to diagnose me. Within a couple weeks, I was able to schedule a physical appointment to get the knot and my symptoms examined.

I didn't realize that being inactive really takes a toll on your body, especially at a youthful age. We were eating healthy, but that wasn't enough. Thankfully, I hadn't developed a serious condition or injury. My body was simply telling me that I needed to get active—*and fast!* While it was still cold outside, I started a daily squat and push-up challenge. As the seasons changed, I switched to walking and biking outside during my lunch hour. Every so often, K.V. joined me. But these activities have become my "me time" or devotional moments. This health scare alone helped me realize that, although K.V. and I are devoted to serving and caring for one another, it is equally as important to tend to our individual personal health. Whether it be mental, physical, spiritual or emotional, self-care should be a consistent area of concern.

So much has transpired during the COVID-19 pandemic. I am grateful for those areas in our life that require some extra care being exposed. As we're celebrating one-year of marriage, I can proudly say that we're not trying to paint a picture of a perfect marriage; yet we want to observe its intricacies and grow together. Throughout this season, I have become much more connected to my husband. We're willing to do the work for a long-lasting partnership and life together. COVID-19 has not broken us! It's tilling the soil in our foundation and plucking out defective seeds.

Marriage Uncut
CHECKPOINT

1. What instance can you recall when you were working against your home rather than yielding to wisdom?

   _____

   _____

2. What have you done to create boundaries and spend quality time with your partner?

   _____

   _____

3. Describe you and your partner's communication styles. How do you collaborate with these differences?

   _____

   _____

4. What habits have you established in your household during this pandemic?

   _____

   _____

5. What does unity mean in your relationship?

   _____

   _____

About the Author
➡ Tiffany Banks

While many people simply consider worship to be something you do, it's the totality of who she is. For Tiffany Banks, affectionately and professionally known as Tiffany Nichole, music is so much more than a great tune and beat. She is intentional about using her God-given gift of singing to shift atmospheres and flow in the prophetic as she ministers with a pure heart—ushering her audiences into an unimaginable spiritual high. Known by some as the "pint-sized powerhouse of praise," Tiffany infuses hope, joy and peace into her music ministry, leaving all who are in attendance inspired to be the best version of themselves.

On a mission to leave this life empty, Tiffany refuses to live a life of fear, never fulfilling what God has called her to do. Aspiring to leave a positive impact on all those who encounter her ministry, she encourages others to embrace their unique abilities, master their identity in Christ and perfect the gifts that God has favored them with to impact the world at-large. She and her husband, K.V. Banks, endeavor to create a new legacy of wealth and generational success, as well as exemplify the true love of God through their marriage.

For booking or interviews, email tnm@tnicholeministries.org. For the latest updates and events, visit tnicholeministries.org.

Mr. & Mrs. Smith:
Let Me Reintroduce Myself
by Ray Shipman

I sat up at 7:45 a.m., after hitting the snooze alarm three times. My feet touched the ground and I was praying in the Holy Ghost. I gathered my belongings and headed to the bathroom to shower and get ready for work. As I stood in the shower worshiping, I realized that I was about to be late for work, *again*. I rushed out and kissed my wife (as is my custom), and I jumped in my car to head to work. As I drove, I listened to the Lord and sang Zion songs.

My phone rang. It was my first client. My day started with a client not being able to get to their doctor's appointment, even though I had already given them bus tickets. By the time I got to work *late*, I had already talked to three clients and my supervisor regarding why I was late. Side note: My supervisor was my pastor, so I was always in prayer about something.

I finally got to my desk, and I had forty-two messages that I hadn't been able to pull off of my voicemail. I was frustrated because I'd already asked to be able to check my voicemail. Staff told me that nobody knew how to check the voicemail. *What do you mean nobody knows how to do it?* My level of frustration rose. As a child, I didn't like when others didn't listen to me. Clearly, I wasn't being heard. I complained to my supervisor, and we discussed a better way to respond than complaining. I expressed the fact that I'm not sure how to respond when I have mentioned it several times already, yet nobody was listening to anything I said.

I checked my work phone, which had five messages from the time I walked into the office to my desk. *How was that even possible?* I pulled my charts out and started working, looking forward to going to lunch. I didn't bring a lunch that day, so I had to figure out what I had a taste for. Next door was a Detroit favorite, a Coney Island. I would go there and get a chicken salad. Actually, I felt more like a pizza, or some chips and cookies. I actually end up grabbing a pop and some fries from the fast-food joint around the corner. I wanted to have it my way and get out of the office.

The day took a huge turn to the left. My supervisor asked for a list of clients who received medication delivered in our office. I already knew that there were only two people. So, I texted it to my supervisor.

He said, "I didn't want you to text it."

"You didn't say how you wanted it. You just wanted the information. You want it typed and double-spaced?"

"Just get it to me," he said.

I made the names seventy-two-point font and turned it in. He was frustrated and told me to go home.

"I'm not going home!"

I went back to my desk and continued to work. I received a text message that told me to report to our other supervisor. I was already over it. I was ready to go home and I didn't want to deal with another face or person.

I remembered that we had two houses. It was the night that my wife was supposed to go over there to check on the kids. With two houses, we had to split our time in between the two houses so that our investments were not destroyed. I met with our director and we got that beef squashed. The only problem was that I was already over the day. I was over people and over life. I just wanted to go home, turn on the television and crawl under the covers until the next day.

I started the day off praying in the spirit. I am a prophet and I serve my church as the senior pastor. I do social work, and this was how I was appreciated? I was over this day. As I headed home, I realized that I could finally breathe. I could shake off the foul stench of the day and just start again the next day.

I got home and my wife had already headed over to the other house so I could take a breather. If she had been there, I would have emptied my day on her. I didn't want to do that. I just wanted to be alone for a little while. The next morning, when my feet hit the floor, I start praying in the Holy Ghost. I headed to the shower to get my day started and I was reminded of a prophetic word God spoke about a virus coming from China and causing death. I shrugged it off and got ready for work. Driving and worshipping, my phone rang. It was my first client.

That morning, I thought of my wife because she had left from our other house and went to work in Ann Arbor. This was our pattern at least two or three days a week. We had to stay in separate houses and wake up in separate beds in order to make sure our houses were taken care of. It was working well since she was working forty-five minutes away. We didn't want to just give the houses away to the kids. Even more, we both enjoyed our alone time. It's not like we didn't like each other. We enjoy each other's company, and we always have.

We were not only friends in high school, but we dated, as well. I actually went to her prom with her. We were supposed to be married right out of high school, but we didn't. She married someone else, so did I. We both had kids, then we divorced. We found each other all over again and, well, here we are, building our relationship. Today, we pastor together. I've been in ministry for over thirty years. I'm now pastoring the church that my father started in 1997. This church enjoyed the leadership of my father for twenty years. Now, I was able to take the helm.

As much as we are alike, we are different. I was adjusting to the life of being a new pastor, as well as the life of a husband. Consistency and stability were necessary for all that was out of order in my life. She was that constant in 1995, and she remains that stability in my life to this day.

We got into a system. We knew what would happen each day and night. We weren't worried about everybody else's idea of what our marriage looked like. We were committed to building. We were building a community, not just a house. This meant we needed to be able to manage us, our properties, as well as our ministries. We didn't take that lightly, but we focused on what we were building. Every morning, it was the same. I was up, praying in the Holy Ghost, hitting the shower, and driving to work. The evening usually ended the same. If she was next to me or not, I was praying in the Holy Ghost on my way to sleep. I know sometimes me being spiritual can be a bit much. But, secretly, I think she loves it.

That morning, some of our staff members were told that they shouldn't come in if they had been sick or had underlying health issues. If we were ever placed in a setting where we may have been exposed to any sickness, we were told to stay at home. We were told later that day that the governor was going to start shutting down things. We were going to beat her to the punch.

My company assisted people who had health mobilities specific to HIV and hepatitis. Some are on medications. This meant we frontline workers were forced to deal with clients who were homeless, prostitutes, "couch surfers" and drug users. This put all of our employees at risk, and my CEO was not having it. She sent us home and told us to not come back until after things cleared. We were told we could work from home. It was great. I didn't have to get up and drive to the office every morning. I thought this would be the perfect opportunity for us to build our lives and refocus. I may have even been able to get a lot more accomplished while working from home, especially since she was working forty-five minutes away. I already planned to wake up late, do some work, put something in the crockpot for dinner, then take a nap. I would watch some more TV and jump in the shower before she got home.

Right after I confirmed my plans for the next couple of weeks, the governor said we needed to quarantine. I wasn't exactly sure what that meant. My wife works in the medical field in a call center, and they weren't closing. They started to define what the essential workers looked like. We weren't on that list. They issued a warning and specifics on what we could and couldn't do. We were also told that we couldn't visit from one house to another. Family visits and neighbor visits were off limits. If you were not an essential worker, you needed to be at home and off the roads.

In all of our building, we didn't consider this. We didn't consider that we would suddenly be put in a place where we would be separated for months. We didn't know how long we would be locked down, nor how long we would be away from our other house. We had to make a choice. I told my wife that she had to choose if she was going to be at this house or the other house because *nobody* could afford a $1,000 ticket for just driving back and forth between the houses. She excitedly said that she would just stay with me. I was happy. We hadn't been able to really spend time together. While we were figuring out how the other house would be monitored and cared for, we found out that she was going to work from home, too.

The excitement was incredible! We could finally work together. We could support each other in the building of the church, our future and the future of our children, together. We had time to work and play together. We had time to plan.

It was like we had been married for the first time again. We stayed up, watching her favorite cop show. We talked about the characters like they were our friends. Then, we watched *Friends* and we ordered pizza. We ate, laughed and worked at home. Two weeks later, I realized that working from home was probably the worst thing I could have ever asked for.

Check out this math:

- 9 hours of work (including lunch)
- 1 hour and 15 minutes of traffic
- 30 minutes in the shower
- 45 minutes of prayer
- 1 hour and 30 minutes of cooking and dinner
- 7 hours of sleep
- 4 hours laughing, talking and watching TV

We literally had about three or four hours of each other's time, face to face, each day. We were literally in each other's face, suddenly spending about fourteen hours with each other daily. I didn't know that she spent this much time on the phone for work. I didn't know that she literally watched SVU all day long. She talked about me eating in the bed. Yet, she had snacks right next to the bed. I didn't know that her opinion was so strong about so much that was happening at the church. Neither of us had done this before (run a church in a pandemic). This was all new. I had stuff that I was trying to process as the pastor and now, as a stay-at-home husband. I had to hear all of the stuff that happens with the church, as well as on her job. I had to hear what was wrong with the house and move the rest of my stuff. Now, she was complaining about my stupid *socks*. Who cared if I left my stupid *socks* on the floor?

I dragged myself out of the bed. I muttered some tongues and a, "Thank you, Jesus" as I headed to the sink. I didn't even feel like getting in the shower. I washed my face and moved forward. I went back into the room and pulled out my laptop. I had to put on my headphones to get to work because she had her headphones on. She didn't realize how loud she was talking. I didn't realize that she talked so loudly either. For dinner, I wanted a home-cooked meal. No one was cooking. She had to work. I was frustrated. This wasn't a vacation; this was torture.

How are we going to survive this?

Our disagreements became more and more specific to the little things. The socks. The TV was too loud. The snacks that we thought were cute before were now frustrating. This ain't got nothing to do with loving her now. This has everything to do with home training. *Why does she chew so loudly?* Our "intense fellowship" became more like passionate "driveness." I mean, we literally drove the other person to the edge of existence and dropped them off. Because our responses are so similar, it was like adding wood to fire. The fire continued to build because we were not used to being this close to each other for so long.

As a couple, we have only been able to exist because of the love and mercy of God, not because of the love that we have for each other. We knew each other before this pandemic. But now, we had to reintroduce ourselves to each other. I had to discover the supervisor (my wife is a lead at her job) and listen to some of the discussions she must have with her staff. I've had to listen to her click on her computer and make all these faces while I say nothing. When I ask, "Is everything okay?" her response comes out as if *I* did something wrong.

I thought this would be a lot easier. We were spending more time together. We were literally forced to be with each other and now, we could barely look at each other. We made a wall of goals in our bedroom. We couldn't really focus on those because we could barely get through a discussion of which one would be easier to accomplish the quickest. The kids were not a discussion because our opinions on what to do and say to them is always different. Even though we spoil all of our kids, we spoil them *differently*. She slept on *this* side; I slept on *that* side.

I couldn't handle the silence. So, I would sit up and watch TV. I tried to talk about it, and she was offended on the approach. I was offended by *her response*. We ended up yelling at each other. I threw a lemon meringue pie across the room, while yelling at the top of my lungs.

This is just the description of *one* fight. At one point, I gathered all of my wife's things and told her to get out and go to *her* house. I got her clothes, her shoes and her snacks, and packed them up and told her to go. I got her "toys" and all her stuff and said, "Take all of it! I don't want to hear, nor see you." She went to the top of the stairs and sat down. I went upstairs and told her that she didn't have to go. This was a stupid argument. I didn't want her to leave. Remember, she was my constant and my stability. But, in that moment, she was pissing me off. The degree of frustration we drove each other to was so extreme that we started to bleed into ministry. We understood that we had a job to do as it pertains to ministry. We couldn't call off our jobs because we got into it with our spouse. So, we refused to just call off when it came to serving God's people. I don't call it being fake; I called it putting your stuff on the backburner to accomplish the goal. Then, we could get back to it after ministry was done. Well, a couple of times, that didn't work.

She showed up to church upset, and it was obvious to several people. I told her when we got home, "If you're going to have an attitude at church, then just stay at home." I told her this not for politics, but because people will follow her lead. If she's bothered, they will be bothered just because of it. One day, she decided to do just that. She stayed at home. Eventually, she did show up to service, but it didn't matter. She did exactly what I asked, which didn't make me happy, either. *Straighten up and do the job!* I guess it's kind of difficult when the entire world is turned upside down and you have to deal with this person who you love— but don't like—for hours on end, and they won't go away.

My parents picked up that something was happening with us. We went to my office to discuss it. I went off. I started yelling and going on and on. She rolled her eyes, which just pissed me off even more. My dad stopped me and asked, "Have you tried to just talk?"

I responded loudly, "I already did!"

He tried to calm me down. My mom sat in the corner, praying and shaking her head. She apologized for not listening to me as a child.

"That's probably why it has become so important for you to be heard," she said.

As they parented and pastored the pastors, my dad, in his simple frustration, asked something ever so small: "Does it work?"

"Does it work? *What do you mean does it work?* You mean when I tried to talk to her, and she didn't listen? I tried to text and that blew up in my face. I called and that was flat and empty. I apologized and that didn't work."

I wasn't getting my point across to any of them in that room. So, I gathered my stuff and said, "I'm not going to sit here and do this. I've tried everything." My dad stopped me.

"Have you? Have you tried *everything?*" my dad asked.

My mind was reeling from all of the emotions and the deception I thought was our future. I didn't even care anymore at that point. I was tired.

In all of his wisdom, my father said to me, "Try something else."

I ran with his words of wisdom and have been running with it for months now. Sometimes, you must *reintroduce* yourself to your spouse. As we grow and change because of life's curveballs, you don't respond or think the same way as you did when you first got married. It makes sense that you would have to have a discussion to say, "I'm thinking this way." I know that it may seem farfetched. But when you are trapped in a house with the person you wanted to spend your life with, but not your every waking second with, you start to think differently. You can either look for the things that are going to make you increasingly mad, or you can reintroduce yourself to the person you are going to spend the rest of your life with.

You are not just in a marriage; you're in a covenant. A covenant goes beyond your likes and dislikes. It minimizes your own opinions and identities about someone else and magnifies your own frailties. It shows that the things that you have built on will change and grow and, if you remain the same, then you're actually *the problem* in your relationship. I have been learning that I have to constantly try something different. I've got to constantly do something differently. I can't just say, "I tried this…," then everything else goes away.

If we are to prosper in our relationship, we must learn who the other person is in the midst of the ups and downs. Remember, we are each other's strength. We are not *just married*. There will be other pandemics. It may not be COVID-19, but there will be other storms we have to encounter. We will feel like we are stuck, and things that we loved at one time will start to get on our nerves and annoy us. Here's what I've learned to do: Try something different at some point.

You will almost always find the right answer.

Marriage Uncut
CHECKPOINT

1. What is your spouse's first response when you, or your spouse, is angry or frustrated?

   _____

   _____

2. Why do you think this is the first response?

   _____

   _____

3. What have you tried to do in order to make sure you can communicate effectively with your spouse?

   _____

   _____

4. In the long list of things that you have tried, what has worked and what hasn't?

   _____

   _____

5. Who are you today, that you weren't last year, and are you willing to reintroduce yourself to your spouse?

   _____

   _____

About the Author
➥ Ray Shipman

Prophet Ray Shipman serves as the senior pastor of Walk in the Sprit Ministries COGIC. He also works in the social work field, specifically mental health for the last fifteen years. He has operated in ministry the last thirty years in several different capacities. He has been fathered in ministry by his natural parents, Pastor Leon K. and Elect-Lady Dian Shipman, as well as Drs. Jerry and Sherill Piscopo. He has served in several areas in ministry, from deliverance, youth and children, to associate pastor, outreach pastor, worship and drama.

He operates heavily in prophetic ministry, as well as in training and equipping the saints. His wife serves with him in ministry as the body life pastor, acting as the eyes and ears for the senior pastor and staying heavily connected to the body of the church. He has several children, both natural and spiritual. Many are connected through his network, EPHOD (Emerging Prophets Heralding Our Destinies). He oversees PRay Ministries (Pronounced P-Ray), that reaches many through his PAT (Prophetic

Activation Trainings). Prophet Ray travels extensively, ministering to the body of Christ with a focus on empowerment, evangelism and encouragement. He has written and published thirteen books, which are all available on Amazon, covering topics such as deliverance and inner-healing, servant leadership and prophetic activations for children and adults, as well as marriage workbooks.

Prophet Ray has a heart for God's people to grow and experience the love and power of God. He believes in transparency in his life and ministry for the development of the life of the believer.

Endless Love
by Nakeya Shipman

Listen! A day in the life of a Shipman is *long*.

First, it's long simply because you are a Shipman. But it's also unpredictable. You can wake up in the morning and believe that all there is to do is work and cook dinner when you get home. However, many days, by the time I am out of the shower, the calendar has been updated five times and there is no *real* room for even work. So, just imagine what it was like when the coronavirus was introduced into my already chaotic life! My bad. Let me rewind so that you can follow this chaos correctly.

I am married to an amazing man who just so happens to be the senior pastor of a church, where I serve as the body life pastor. As the body life pastor, I serve the members. I check in with them when they are missing in action, and I support them on a consistent basis. This allows our senior pastor to focus on building the vision, while I help build the people and push the heart of the vision into our members. We both work full-time, in the secular world and in ministry. We have children. We both write. We both are in school. And did I mention that we have to do life counseling and coaching at our regular jobs, in our church and to a host of other folks that we don't even really know? Then, we were thrown into COVID-19.

We have two homes, one east and one west. My schedule usually determines which location I stay at. This agreement has worked for us for the last two years. However, due to the pandemic, and the fear of it possibly being a complete shutdown, we agreed to stay at one location. Although we have been married two years, I was terrified about what would happen if we had to deal with each other every day. I know you are thinking, "That's what husbands and wives do daily." Well, not *this* husband and wife duo. We had a system. Without the coronavirus, the system was moving along simply fine. At least, that's what I kept telling myself.

I literally lost my mind for a few reasons. My routine was changing and now, I would lose control. When I am angry and don't want to be bothered, I no longer have a safe place that will cover me. My brain was in panic mode and my heart was overwhelmed. When we said, "I do!", we agreed to only occupy the two homes for two years. At the end of the second year, we hadn't changed the routine. We hadn't even thought about it any further. Then, the Lord sent a reminder of our covenant agreement. I tried to hold out and see how things were going to go. I received a call from my oldest son though.

"Mom, I'm just going to stay in my dorm until this thing passes over. The school said that we would have the ability to stay with everything that is going on."

Of course, like any other mother, I called the school to verify that the information that I received from my son was correct. They confirmed that he could stay on campus. They were practicing all of the suggested safety measures. This was good news, at first. He was staying at the dorm, so there was still space for my younger son to come home without making the house crowded. But two days later, he called me back to say that he had to be out the next day. Things at that point escalated. There was little to no time to plan or figure things out. This was the move that caused me to *have* to honor the commitment and vow that I had made before the Lord. The next day, I packed up and picked up both of my sons. They both had tons of stuff. The only thing left to do was for me to move my stuff out and move their stuff in.

The first few nights felt normal because we have always spent at least four consecutive days a week under one roof. I thought to myself in those first few days, *You got this, champ! What were you afraid of?* I made it through the first week strong and vibrant, looking forward to each new day with my husband. The second week came, and I thought I had it by the ears. I was in full control. By the time I'd made it to Friday, I was *lost*. I was trying to figure out what was changing. I hadn't done anything differently. He hadn't done anything differently. But, for some reason, it seemed like we were both just getting on the other person's *very last nerve* for no good reason.

Every day became longer. I felt like I was being punished for something that someone else had done. My anger became sadness and frustration. It seemed like, no matter what we tried, we couldn't hear one another. Week four came. At that point, I felt like I needed to escape. This constant time was driving me *crazy*.

Prior to the coronavirus outbreak, I wanted every minute of my husband's time. I looked forward to every moment when we were together. When we were at separate houses, I would text all day and all night about how I missed my "cuddle buddy." With me being with him every single day now, I no longer missed him. My feelings of missing him now transformed into frustration, anger and even *rage*.

I had to figure out what was happening. What was the cause of the frustration and all of the emotions? What was I *really* tired of? I kept trying to pinpoint what was causing the triggers to go off. My tolerance for the man I love was short. I started watching his behavior and my responses to those behaviors. I couldn't pinpoint what was happening, *nor* why it was happening. I decided to pray about it and see what God would show me about myself. I had to fix whatever was happening.

I was struggling in my prayer because I needed an answer immediately. I felt like God was ignoring me. I started to take it personal. I had to talk to God out of desperation, so I thought that He could understand that this need was *urgent*. Even in my urgency, I didn't feel like He had said anything that would assist me with my marriage. I kept going back to the Lord to seek answers. Just when I thought I was done asking God, and when I was just going to pack up and leave, that was the very moment when the Lord dropped a bomb on me.

"Just as you have felt ignored, your husband hasn't felt heard. I needed to show you what it felt like in order for you to understand. Even though you are present, he feels unheard which, in turn, makes him feel ignored. When you talk to me as my daughter, you expect that I hear you and I respond. You must make the same concession for your husband as you expect him to do for you."

At that moment, I had the ability to see that my husband needed his wife. Even with the few days that we had apart, he still needed and wanted his *wife*. He didn't feel like I could hear his heart or his needs because I was always trying to fix things—not realizing they were only symptoms of what our true issue was. I felt terrible that, as his wife, I had been missing one of the key things that I had been fighting about. I purposed in my heart to do better.

The first week after my revelation, I was excited and ready to show off what the Lord had shown me. I didn't tell my husband because I wanted to *show* him. I tried to make sure that I listened and that my responses weren't sharp or guarded. I tried to lower my tone, so I didn't come across as angry or mad. I thought I was doing a good job.

Then, he burst my bubble.

In the middle of an intense fellowship (what we call our arguments), he reminded me of how, when I lower my tone, it sounds condescending. When I think I am attentively listening, it looks like I am actively ignoring him. Here I was thinking that I was doing what he needed. Even in my effort, he still thought I was rude, condescending and even, at times, disrespectful. This news was heartbreaking. I thought I was doing much better. And, of course, now I had a billion and one things going through my head. *Does he want someone else? Is he just tired of me being around? Do I need to just leave and allow him his own space?* Although I had many questions, I didn't have an answer to any of them.

I decided that I wanted to change the tone of our marriage. We were best friends before we were anything else. We needed to find our way back to friendship. We needed to relocate the love that we always had for each other. We had a sit-down, heart-to-heart talk where we both shared our fears, our needs and our desires. We had missed a lot. We'd taken for granted that we have known each other for over twenty-four years. We didn't look to get to know the *new* person. We just judged one another based on who they used to be. We agreed to be friends and to withhold nothing from one another.

Each day got better. Throughout the day, we texted one another just to say, "Hello," or just to send small simple gestures of love. I started crushing on him all over again. As the weeks went by, we challenged each other to keep doing just that so we could continue to grow. We realized that we needed to refresh our views in order to see the heart of the other person. Now that we were back on track, and planning to buy a house, we started creating our goal wall. We placed all of our family goals on the wall in our room so we could always see where we are in the process.

Our reconnection as friends caused every area of our marriage to thrive. Our communication with one another changed. We connected on a deeper level in the spirit, and we became even more connected when it came to intimacy. Changing our viewpoint allowed us to see into the heart of one another. Seeing the heart of my husband, and what he desires to do for me and our family, caused me to be even more attracted to him. I longed for his hugs, his kisses and his cuddling daily.

Intimacy becomes blocked when you aren't communicating or seeing eye to eye. So, for a while, we struggled. I wanted to go to sleep, and he wanted to watch TV. So, we both made it about the *other stuff* versus identifying that our inability to communicate and deal with each other every day was impacting our ability to be intimate with one another. Once we were able to communicate with one another, and we were able to share with one another the secrets of our hearts, it opened up our passion for one another. We went from talking about business and the church, to talking about what we liked, what we wanted and how we wanted it. We made new commitments to one another and to God. We agreed to be intentional in our marriage and to being intimate every day. We don't always succeed daily, but we make sure that we make up for the days we miss.

One of the best parts of being friends with your spouse is that you know all the secrets. So, role playing is easy.

Being at home the majority of the time has given us the ability to explore. We set up dates like we are different people. We have spent hours texting one another about the nasty things we want to do to one another. This may not seem like a big deal. But, for me, it's a huge deal. I was molested as a child, and I dreaded intimacy for a long time. I didn't like to be touched. I was okay with being intimate once or twice a month. The shutdown allowed me to take off my shell and open up my heart. It allowed me to give all of the pieces to my world to my husband. His strength in some of the things I had experienced created an attraction. Every word he spoke made me want him *more*. He made me feel safe and secure, so my body longed to just be in his arms.

Getting past being violated as a child was something I repeatedly tried to do. There was no real release until my husband and I had to spend every day together. We became best friends all over again. This caused him to see me, and me to hear him, which knitted us together. Our hearts found each other in a way that we had never experienced. We were like kids all over again. When he entered the room, I became like a little girl all over again. My heart skipped beats. My stomach turned before he even acknowledged my presence. Once he laid eyes on me, his amazing smile lit up my world. And, as corny as it sounds, I look forward to it every day. The spark of passion has now become a constant flame. Being apart seems like something is missing simply because of a lockdown. I thought everything changed because of the pandemic. Then, I received a revelation.

It wasn't about coronavirus. It was about God stripping us down so that we could be transparent with one another. When I got that revelation, I was excited. We are transparent and we share everything with one another. I was missing it though. It wasn't just about us being transparent. It was about our ability to access where we were and what we needed in order for our covenant to thrive.

As life would have it, we had a good thing going for a while. Even when small foxes came, we worked together to eliminate or alleviate the damage. Then suddenly, I felt insecure and left out. He was always gone all of a sudden. I rarely got a chance to see his face, other than to say, "I love you" and "Good night." I began to speculate. I felt uneasy about being alone. I couldn't take any more heartache or disappointment. I didn't want to accuse him of anything, but I felt like I was losing— not just my husband—but my best friend and lover.

I sank into a depression. I felt unworthy. I didn't feel important. I was an afterthought. I struggled with how I would bring this to my husband's attention, without it becoming a big deal. I didn't want him to think I was nagging. I didn't want him to feel forced into being bothered with me. I struggled extremely hard here because I'd also promised him that I would process my feelings faster. I had promised to let him know about whatever was bothering me immediately. That was much harder than I thought. Even though we had reconnected, and we were back in our state of being best friends, me exposing to him how he'd hurt me or made me feel seemed like such a fragile place. I wasn't sure I could do that. This was different than me just exposing who I am, what I like and where I was headed. I had to expose how he'd hurt me and put me in a vulnerable position, which caused me to feel like I was weak.

With all of this going on in my head, I felt like I couldn't show him any sign of weakness. I refused to show him that I wanted him home with me, even if it was just doing nothing. To me, that said to him that I was weak. I didn't want him to know the impact he'd had on my heart, my world and everything that is connected to me. I needed to be able to share this with him, but my *pride* kept giving me reasons why I shouldn't. Since this was something that wasn't just going to go away, I prayed. I asked God for direction and understanding. The Lord directed me to my mom.

I called her and expressed to her that she had only taught me to be strong. She'd never taught me how to be weak enough to share my heart. I needed for her, at that moment, to lend me support in order to come out of a place and be what I hadn't ever known in that way. She gave me the best advice a mother could give: "Trust your husband, not just with your greatness, but also trust him in covering and protecting you, even from him."

I needed to understand how I would give him the weak and damaged pieces of my heart in order for us to tear down this wall, which was built solely off emotions, which can change at any second. I needed to find out what I needed to do—and quickly—before my emotional outbursts drove my husband out the front door. I settled in understanding that I had nothing to lose, but everything to gain.

My marriage couldn't die in the middle of a pandemic. I needed to figure out quickly what I needed to do. I needed to know how to implement it so that my husband knew that I love him and that our marriage matters to me. I made sure that, no matter what it was, I said it to my husband. The times where I felt abandoned and left behind, I made sure that I shared it with him. I shared with him how I felt and how his actions have made me feel. In those moments, I felt like I was struggling with where and how I fit into his life. I was searching for a place where I was larger than the thing in his heart. It seemed like I couldn't find a space. It seemed like the intense "fellowship" was hotter than ever before.

I said I was leaving. He was okay with it, and he packed my stuff *for* me.

I was hurt at first. Then, I became *angry. How does he feel like it is okay for him to pack up my stuff when he was the one who was wrong?* The one who forgot he had a wife. Our makeup was always to exit because we've always had a second home. This time, though, we chose to talk and have the difficult conversation. The conversation became heated, as usual. We both paused and it was almost immediately that we understood that we were allowing the chaos. We realized that it was no longer in the hands of the enemy, but that we were allowing emotions and things that we can control to keep us divided.

I apologized immediately for not making sure he was heard. I apologized for the times he needed to be heard and I didn't hear him because of my own issues. That's when I said to him, "I just want to fit into your life and feel that I'm important." I let go of my fear and just let him see my pain and vulnerability. It seemed like, at that moment, he didn't hear me though. I felt like he'd brushed it off and I was just expected to move on.

Right as I was about to walk away and go into my place of safety (shutdown mode), my husband stopped me. He grabbed my hand and said, "Honey, you don't fit in my world." What I heard him say was, "There is no more room in my world for you." Before the first tear could reach my nose, he said, "You are *first* in my world." Those simple words consumed my heart and allowed me to breathe. I planted my head in his chest and shed my few tears. I hugged him as he held me in his arms. At that moment, I felt safer than I had in my entire life. This hug reaffirmed his strength in my weakness, and it took me back to the place of falling in love.

We have endured tears, frustration, disagreement and miscommunication malfunctions. We are still here, still together, still growing, still dedicated and finding new ways to show our love to one another. We war hard and we are passionate about many things. However, we make sure now that we war just as hard for one another and for our time together as we did against each other in the past. We are working to be intentional with one another in all things. We will come out of this pandemic more in love, more connected and more committed to one another. We have found our friendship, our passion and our forever love.

"Intense fellowships" still occur; however, we aren't enemies to one another. We are a team that fights fair and loves hard. We forgive quickly and take our time making up. We have conquered our fears in the face of a pandemic. We've gained tools to ensure that we are fighting fair. We have fought hard, but we have loved harder. We have written books. We have started launching other areas of business. We fell in love with one another all over again.

We will always remain, #myforeverlove.

Marriage Uncut
CHECKPOINT

1. How would you have handled trying to fit into the chaotic life of your spouse?

   _____
   _____

2. How do you connect intimately with your spouse when you both are consumed with busy schedules?

   _____
   _____

3. Without neglecting your responsibilities, how do you make time for your spouse?

   _____
   _____

4. What communication tools do you use in your marriage to overcome misunderstandings?

   _____
   _____

5. How do you determine what issues to bring to your spouse?

   _____
   _____

About the Author
➥ Nakeya Shipman

Nakeya Nichol Shipman, charismatically known as Pastor Nakeya or Lady K, is the founder of Level Up Ministries, Created in His Image (Ministry Realistically) and also the body life pastor at Walk in The Spirit Ministries. Nakeya serves in many capacities. She is a certified coach, supervisor in the marketplace and a leader in ministry. A committed worker who is dedicated to the growth and development of all she touches, she is a force to be reckoned with. In 2013, Nakeya returned to her hometown of Detroit after relocating and being gone over sixteen years. Shortly after her return, she married her high-school sweetheart and first love, Ray Shipman. She works alongside her husband to build people and ministries to ensure that kingdom work is always being done.

Love & Basketball
by Celeste Blackman

When we look at our troubles from our perspective, we're filled with dread and anxiety. At the time, they may seem insurmountable. That's when we need to hand them over to God. He has all the power, strength and wisdom to handle all things. For our worries, He's already created a solution—one which we've never even considered. He even reminds us to worry less and pray more.

Philippians 4:6-7 (NIV) says, *Do not be anxious about anything, but in every situation, by prayer and petition, with thanksgiving, present your requests to God. And the peace of God, which transcends all understanding, will guard your hearts and your minds in Christ Jesus.* Prayer isn't optional; it's mandatory. I had a foundation and knew the importance of prayer previously, but I allowed interference and disorder to disrupt the pattern. Many times, I lost focus due to my own understanding. God definitely knew what He was doing when He told me to stop and be still.

Prior to COVID-19, my marriage was pretty rocky. I had a lot going on personally that did not have anything to do with my marriage. I had become part of many great organizations that were pulling me in so many different directions. Unaware of how much involvement it would all take, I jumped in headfirst. I became way too busy, thinking I had it all under control. I didn't do much research or consider my husband's thoughts. Every time an opportunity presented itself, I jumped on it. I didn't ask my husband's opinion or even consider if he had one. It didn't matter to me. It was my time, and his voice didn't matter—so I thought.

Being married for twenty-three years and still operating as though I was single was a sin from the pit of hell. Eventually, I realized what I was doing. There were plenty of days when my business partners thought I was crazy. When they asked me a simple question, such as, "Who are you? What service do you offer? And what problems do you solve?" my mind was cluttered. Many times, I couldn't answer. Even when I did, it came out as gibberish. No solid description or foundation at all. I would walk away, feeling stupid and beating myself up. I felt like a total loser.

There was no room left. I couldn't allow anything else in because I had absorbed so much information between trainings, meetings and everything in between that I wasn't doing anything with it. I didn't apply any of it. None of it had to do with what should've been considered in the first place.

Maybe that's why I struggled with much because it was all being done out of order. Having order in your life is everything. From praising God to counting your fingers, if it needs to be aligned, line it up. When you have order, everything else will fall in line—until I realized I had done it again. I'd taken on everything yet released nothing. I was lost.

I lost focus of what was important. I always knew the spiritual order with Christ, God, family, then everything else. However, I got so busy that I couldn't think straight. I would tend to everyone and everything else, then God and family got in where they fit in (if they fit at all). I couldn't focus, even when I spoke. It caused me great harm because what I spoke wasn't what my mind was saying. Every time I opened my mouth, I sounded foolish, even when it came to my household. My attitude was horrible. I was cursing more than normal and eating ridiculously. My attitude was disrespectful. In April of 2019, the Lord spoke to me as clear as the ray of sun on a summer morning.

He said, "Stop!"

I asked myself, "Stop? Huh?"

At that time, I had four events planned. I was in the midst of planning another and He was telling me to stop! At that time, I could not place my hand on my keyboard to type anything. Every time I attempted to type, I couldn't do it. I started to question God, although I knew better. But

I needed to know why. I mentally started asking God a series of questions. *Why are you stopping me, God? These people are depending on me. I need to do this. I need to accomplish this. I have people waiting on me.* So many thoughts raced through my mind as I fought back tears.

At the same time, my husband was depending on me. He needed me. We had goals we needed to accomplish. My husband waited at home for me many late nights while I was doing everything for everyone else. I was great for helping others with their businesses while neglecting what I needed to do for my husband and me. So, I did just that.

I stopped!

During that season, I didn't know what to expect. I didn't know what was. I didn't know why. All I knew was that God said, "Stop!" and I needed to follow His direction. I had truly become distracted. I'd lost focus of who I was, whose I was, and what I was supposed to be doing. So, during that time, I simply stopped. I'd become so overwhelmed during that season of my life that my marriage was failing. I'd made decisions personally for my life, and not *our life*. Being disobedient caused much strife in my marriage. The weight of my choices was overwhelming. Yet, I blamed my husband.

I would say things like, "You don't hug me!" or "We don't have sex enough!" or even "You don't do this or that!" I sounded like a broken record: "You, you, you, you, you!" I kept doing what I *wanted* to do, instead of what I was *supposed* to be doing. I felt like I needed intimacy and attention from my husband more than he needed it from me, only to find out that we both needed the same thing. So often, we misdiagnose our situations by being selfish and inconsiderate. We take advantage of one another. Some knowingly, some unknowingly. There were even times when he attempted to love on me, and I'd shut him down. Because my husband loves to be intimate with me on every level, I sometimes shut him down because I was "tired." I'd also allowed so much and so many other things (and people) to interfere in my life. I caused a lot of strife in my marriage.

I often rejected my husband for sex. I was tired and I didn't feel like it. I would nudge him away every time he went to embrace me with a hug or kiss. At the time, it was small to me. But it meant the world to him. All he would ever do is walk away with frustration, and I didn't care one bit. I was so angry and aggravated some days that I couldn't even speak to him. Even when I spoke, it was nasty, harmful and demeaning to my husband. I soon found that I needed him for everything—even those things I did not include him in.

My husband is a realist. If I wanted something, and I knew he'd decline, I knew how to manipulate the situation.

I can look at him with a straight face and get what I want. I wanted to do what I wanted to do, and get what I wanted to get, and that's what I did. What's amazing is that I allowed my work and desire for building wealth to have total power over me—until it almost ruined all that I had worked so hard for.

I was inconsiderate about my union and the vows we'd taken. So many things transpired between the time God asked me to stop and the time COVID-19 appeared. My husband and I were barely having sex, maybe once a month. We spoke often, but never about us and never about the brick-and-mortar we had built for the last twenty-three years. I would sit and listen to him speak about his day at work with so much frustration. Yet, I wouldn't say a word. I knew my husband wouldn't discuss the elephant in the room. I soon found out that, to him, it was *no elephant*.

I had high expectations that he would do exactly what I needed him to do. I never considered that maybe he was only able to give me what he was given. So often we expect people to give us 100% when, in reality, they can only give us 60% or 70%. They can't heal us from something they have no clue about because we don't tell them. They can't fix something they didn't break. It's up to us to either accept the percentage they have to offer, or let it go.

Even years down the line, I still expected more from him. I found myself many days, asking, "Oh, my goodness! Is he not paying attention? Is he not listening?" Once I voiced my concerns, he received the feedback and the communication rebooted itself immediately. We can't always expect people to know what we need personally without telling them. We can't assume our spouse knows what we need if we've never told them. We should express our needs and our wants. I honestly believe in teaching people how to treat me. But nobody ever taught me those principles. I had to learn on my own. I inquired of my husband to take the journey with me. Although I knew the importance of it, he didn't. There were some things I needed to bring to his attention. Those were my *needs*.

I sometimes felt that I needed much more than I had worked hard to get. In my marriage, I require that silently. Once I came to realize that I had gone through a lot. After having three ectopic pregnancies within ten months, I'd had two surgeries, of which my last ectopic surgery almost caused me to die. I became my father's guardian and stopped all programming for my organization I didn't realize how exhausted I was until I *stopped*.

Thank you, COVID-19. COVID made me *stop*. Plain and simple.

I realized at that time that I had been running non-stop. If I didn't stop soon, my marriage would be on the line. From January 16 through February 9, I was really sick. I can't say that I had COVID-19 because they officially diagnosed me with the flu. However, I knew my body. It had been through a lot due to me running around, not taking care of myself. I didn't pay attention to my body. I didn't allow myself to physically heal. I felt good on the outside. But, internally, I was still bleeding and wounded.

I was diagnosed with flu-like symptoms. But because I've been diagnosed with asthma, it was an exceedingly difficult time for me. I was continuously on steroids. It took me approximately three and a half weeks to heal to actually be able to function fully. I was not hospitalized, or but my body was clearly ill. I totally understood why God stopped me. Not only was my life on the line, but other people's lives are on the line because I am a personal development coach. There was no way I would be able to coach anyone with the exhaustion I had put upon myself and my marriage. I was burned out.

I decided to cultivate *calm*. Psalm 131:2 (NIV) says, *But I have calmed and quieted myself, I am like a weaned child with its mother; like a weaned child I am content*. When I decided to just be quiet, be still and stop, many questioned my decision. They didn't understand how I could stop when it was money to be made. They didn't understand when I turned down opportunities. I found myself explaining my "why" to people who weren't married and didn't understand the spiritual concept. I literally had to tell people, "No, not at this time. I'm focusing on my family." I went from having ten things on my plate to having three or four things on my plate. Yet, that plate still seemed full. I felt like I couldn't absorb another piece from my plate.

Then came the pandemic. It forced not only me, but many, to simply *stop*. When this pandemic first started, it was so sad to me. There were so many people who were so sick and so many people who had lost loved ones. The world just seemed to be so sad. In the midst of the sadness, a light went off. I actually thanked God for COVID-19. Although it brought great sadness to my heart, I found myself being overly grateful. It forced me to be still and to stay in the house. I folded clothes that were piled up to the ceiling. I dusted my furniture and every piece of glass in my house. Most of all, I needed to be pleased with my marriage. During this season, my husband and I became remarkably close.

Sex became a part of our regularly scheduled program again. We shared the chores, decluttered our house, played games and smooched on each other like we were teenagers. I cooked daily, like a sous chef at the fanciest restaurant. Our conversations became wiser and more in-depth. Instead of talking *at each* other and running out the door to do work, we stayed still and had a conversation openly, honestly and willingly. We hug more. We kiss more and we appreciate each other more. When he cleaned up and I messed up, I made sure I cleaned it back up. I took time to consider all that he does, and he did the same. Doing that brought great pleasure to us both. We were so busy with life that we'd lost focus on what was important.

We had been married for twenty-three years at that time COVID-19 hit the world. Maybe we'd both gotten comfortable with our marriage and forgot about the important things. We'd lost the things that kept us close and united as one. I realized that I had to do some things differently.

I started praying and meditating. I sought God for understanding. I put the important things in the correct order. I have regained my position as a wife, putting God first, then my family, and then everything else. Psalms 127:1-2 (NIV) says, *Unless the Lord builds the house, the builders labor in vain. Unless the Lord watches over the city, the guards stand watch in vain. In vain you rise early and stay up late, toiling for food to eat—for he grants sleep to those he loves.* When I read that, I was completely blessed. This Scripture lets me know that God likes you to use the gifts with which you've been blessed. I thank God for reminding me that nothing is too hard for Him.

Many days, I have had thoughts of walking away from my marriage. I never considered the fact that my husband never knew what I needed. *I never told him!* It also reminded me to take those concerns to God and ask Him to be the center of our marriage. I know that He can handle anything and everything. Once I gave my concerns to God, He helped me fix my thoughts on those things that deserve my praise and focus.

Hebrews 11:1 (NIV) says, *Now faith is confidence in what we hope for and assurance about what we do not see. I stopped worrying.* I started to see all that God has promised to come to pass.

When you're going through a hard time, there is only one place you can find comfort: in God's Word. God saved my marriage through COVID-19. My marriage has been renewed and restored by the Word of life. Psalm 119:49-50 (NIV) says, *Remember your word to your servant, for you have given me hope. My comfort in my suffering is this: Your promise preserves my life.*

Today, I am so grateful to say that, just as any other marriage, my marriage has seen some good times and some bad times. But overall, we stand strong. We stand united. We fight for our marriage and we are thankful for COVID-19. It truly saved our marriage and brought us closer as a union.

I've learned many lessons during the pandemic. Many situations came upon during the quarantine.

My father died in April of 2020. Prior to him passing, my husband was still right by my side. I developed a deeper respect for him. I had lost my mom seven years prior and I looked at my husband in a different way. He had truly become my everything all over again, but even more.

I was so grateful that he stood by my side. as But, for some reason, this time was different. It made me realize that, for the first time in my life, he was all I had. The reality of that brought tears, humbleness, restoration, appreciation and abundant love for this man who I had taken advantage of many days. I fell in love all over again. In all things I do and go through, I do so in decency and in order. I will submit unto my husband and to God. God has been faithful through it all. God has shown me during this quarantine not to question Him and not to worry about a thing. I learned to allow my husband to lead and to shut up and *listen!*

COVID-19 saved my marriage!

Marriage Uncut
CHECKPOINT

1. Explain a time you were operating out of your own understanding and it affected your marriage.

   _____

   _____

   _____

   _____

2. Write down a situation when you noticed your spouse desired the same thing as you and how it made you feel.

   _____

   _____

   _____

   _____

3. Have you ever manipulated a situation in your marriage to get what you want? Explain!

   _____

   _____

   _____

   _____

CHECKPOINT, *continued*

4. Other than COVID-19, why else do you think you were to be still in that season?

___

5. What can you do personally or more of in order to maintain your marriage?

___

6. How important do you think it is to ask God to give you and your spouse what you need to save or maintain your marriage?

___

About the Author
➥ Celeste Blackman

What many would consider to be a state of brokenness, Celeste Blackman used as building blocks for success. From sexual abuse and the loss of her mother, to the loss of other family members to gun violence, Celeste knows firsthand what it's like to be broken—mentally, spiritually and emotionally. Using her personal experience as a weapon of warfare to fight for others, she has made it her life's purpose to assist children and adults alike who have lost their parents and feel hopeless. Through a supportive, structured process, she not only positions clients to live a successful, fruitful life—but she teaches them to lead others into a life of fulfillment.

Through 24-hour access to her programs, her clients experience authentic healing and wholeness that they once thought they'd never find. As a counselor and coach to many, Celeste works diligently to make sure her clients feel safe, encouraged and confident when they leave her presence. Having obtained her educational experience from The CAPP Institute for Coaching and Positive Psychology led her to be a highly sought-after partner for many organizations. In addition to serving on the advisory board of Adams Butzel Recreation Complex, she's been fortunate to collaborate with Women Creating Caring Communities, Sow a Seed Youth Organization and Women of Virtue, to name a few.

When she's not helping others move their missions forward in and around the local community, she's busy hosting her signature programs, such as the I Choose 2Win youth mentoring program, Millennial Ladies with Visions and her Easter Disco. Annually, Celeste also organizes a back-to-school rally, a holiday meal program and a women's retreat. Her work as a personal development coach, community activist and woman of influence also led her to be awarded the Spirit of Detroit Award, as well as the "Doin' Good in the Hood" Award.

Today, Celeste moves change forward through The Healing & Prosperity Foundation, which speaks for itself. Through the organization and year-round events, she works to help others heal from the inside out. She fills gaps of poverty with pieces of prosperity, eventually positioning people to help others soar beyond their circumstance or environment. In a world of chaos and confusion, she makes it a point to be the calm of someone's storm—balancing the scales of others so they can maintain mental stability at all times, in all seasons.

For interviews, speaking engagements or more information on upcoming events, email healingandprosperityfoundation@yahoo.com or follow Healing & Prosperity Foundation on Facebook.

Do the Right Thing
by Ortavia McClain

Awakened by the 3 a.m. alarm, I got up to get ready for work on February 26, 2020. I packed my lunch, grabbed my coffee, and kissed my husband Robert as he saw me out to the garage. I was praying on my way to work and feeling good, knowing I only had one more day left to go before my weekend began. Around the 1 p.m. afternoon break, I felt weak. My throat started hurting, and my body started aching. Right before my twelve-minute break was over, I called Robert and told him how I was feeling. He told me he would stop by CVS and pick me up some Theraflu and cough drops. By the time that the 3:30 bell rang, I was at the front door, heading to the gate to clock out of the plant. Once the cold air hit my face, my throat felt like someone had lit a match to it. I got to my truck, cleaned off the snow, and kept praying.

"By His stripes, I'm healed!" I prayed.

I didn't know if I was about to die or not, the way I was feeling. Once I made it home safely, I took my shower and called in sick for the next day. I took the Theraflu that

Robert had bought for me and went to bed. When I woke up hours later, my body was still hurting. So, I made a cup of tea, took a Tylenol, and went back to bed.

"How are you feeling?" Robert asked me the next morning.

"I'm okay. I don't want to go to emergency."

He started getting ready for work as he gave me a kiss.

"I'll check on you later. Call me if you need me to leave work," he said.

Ten hours later, Robert came home from work. He was coughing and his body was aching.

"Whatever I have, I'm sure you have it, too," I said.

I made us some Theraflu and soup. He took a shower and we went to bed. For the next couple of days, I stayed home; but Robert still went to work although he wasn't feeling well. He wasn't feeling as bad as I was. When I woke up, I called my doctor's office and made an appointment.

"I think I may have the flu," I told the receptionist.

When I arrived, the nurse took my vitals. I took a flu test, which came back negative. She gave me a steroid shot, a penicillin shot and some antibiotics to take for the next seven days.

I started feeling better by the fifth day from leaving the doctor's office, but I was still off work. Our son was out of school for winter break. He was over his sister's house, while Robert and I were home, sick. After being off work for almost two weeks, I finally went back to work on March 9th. It was good to be back and I felt a lot better.

On my first day back, one of my coworkers told me that a lot of other people called in sick *the same week* I was off work. By the time that the 11 a.m. lunch bell rang, I was watching the news on my cell phone. Channel 4 News was reporting that the DDOT bus drivers were refusing to pick up passengers due to the coronavirus that was spreading. Then, they announced that the three casinos in downtown Detroit would be closing by the end of the week. Hospitals were overflowing with patients. At this point, it became a little scary for me and some of my coworkers. The casinos were closing, yet the automotive plant still had us working. They hadn't even addressed the breaking news.

On March 18th, I took the day off work. Around 7:30 a.m., my phone was ringing off the hook with messages and notifications from my coworkers. They refused to touch the trucks, which led to other departments refusing to touch the trucks for fear of their health and safety. This automictically stops the line from moving. With the line unable to run, Fiat Chrysler Automobiles (FCA) sent everyone home. But the news reported that the workers walked out, which was not true. This was the beginning of being homebound with hubby.

I called Robert and told him what happened at my plant. Unfortunately, they were still working at his plant. They hadn't even addressed the issue. Hours after Robert got home from work, his supervisor called him and told him not to report to work due to the fact that they were shutting down the plant. After working seven days for the last two months or so, Robert was glad. We both were happy because now, we didn't have to wake up early. We could spend some time together to get some things done around the house and have some much-needed family time.

A week later, our son came back home from his sister's house. We didn't have to go to work, and he didn't have to go to school due to the stay-at-home order issued by Governor Whitmer.

The Outside Boundary

The first two weeks of being at home seemed a little awkward. We all woke up at different times. Our sleep patterns were way off. I would either be in the bedroom watching TV, or in the office checking emails and paying bills. Robert and our son were in the basement watching TV or playing the video game. Sometimes, our son would be in his room on his phone. This wasn't what I pictured a homestay would be like. It started to feel like we were roommates, instead of a family. So, I suggested we watch a movie on PureFlix together. Robert agreed and told our son we would watch a movie around 5 p.m. But my son declined our offer. When Robert and I got ready to go watch the movie in the basement, our son came upstairs and went into his room with his cell phone.

Within thirty minutes of us watching the movie, our son texted Robert, asking him to come upstairs because he had to ask him something. Robert didn't reply right away. So, my son called for him to come upstairs.

"No! You come to me!" Robert yelled.

Ten minutes later, Robert told me, "Pause the movie." He went upstairs to see what our son wanted. Next thing I heard was Robert fussing. I went upstairs to see what the problem was. Our son had called his grandmother to pick him up so he could go over there. We were in the midst of a pandemic and a stay-at-home order! My husband was highly upset, and I felt like we were becoming pandemic parents of a teenager who wasn't taking this seriously.

Robert explained to him that this wasn't a joke and that he wasn't just on a vacation from school.

"We were just sick a few weeks ago," Robert told him. "We don't know if we've had it or not." He told us the reason why he wanted to go with his grandmother, and we understood that. But it was bad timing. He didn't know who else would be over his grandmother's house who could possibly be infected.

"I miss my family, too. But I would rather we all be safe than have to deal with a family member getting the coronavirus and we can't be with them at all," I told him.

"If you go over there, you must stay for two weeks," Robert told him.

He decided to go anyway. He called his grandmother to pick him up. I headed back downstairs. Robert came down afterward and we started talking about what had happened.

"For us to parent him, we must be on the same page and reading from the same book," I said. "So, situations like this don't just happen, especially without our knowledge, at the last minute. We must do what is right and in the best interest for our health and wellbeing."

"He's gonna be gone for two weeks, and he will be back. Then, we don't have to worry about him asking to go again until the stay-at-home order is lifted," he said.

I went back upstairs to get something to drink, and I heard a car horn blow in the driveway. I told him his grandmother was outside as he approached the kitchen with his backpack and X-Box.

He said, "Bye."

I told him, "Bye. Be safe."

He opened the side door, looked toward the basement where his dad was, and said nothing. He just went out the door. I had a feeling that things were about to get worse. Trying to parent in a pandemic with a teenager who was not used to being told, "No!" was more than a notion. When our son finally came back home, he seemed distant from Robert and I. Due to the stay-at-home order, we watched church service on Facebook Live and had bible study on the conference call line. When it was time for church or bible study, my son would sit on the couch with his phone or fall asleep. Robert had to tell him to put his phone up and pay attention many times.

We prayed and took communion together, as well. We also took turns reading the Scriptures. It still didn't feel like we were a family. It felt more like we were roommates. I believe our son was going through something by transitioning and coming to live with us again. Being on the stay-at-home order started to affect him heavily, which made Robert feel like he needed to do more to make him happy. This was the beginning of the end of pandemic parenting. Shortly after he came back, he left again.

He wanted to spend Easter with his family.

Robert told him, "You have to stay over there until the coronavirus is over because you're not taking this serious! You can't live house to house!" He agreed to stay over there. The next couple of days, Robert was a little sad. He wanted to have his son with him, but he didn't want to force him into living with us. I noticed that Robert spent more time watching TV in the basement or on Facebook. My daughter started a group chat with me and my children since we were homebound. I missed them and my grandbabies. It also helped pass the time daily. I started reading my Bible and praying more, if I wasn't watching TV, on Facebook, or in the office on the computer paying bills. Robert seemed to get lost in his phone on the Nike website and Facebook. Periodically, I went to the basement stairs and asked if he was okay or what he was watching. We like to watch different shows. He likes sports and sci-fi movies, while I like the family shows, Christian and drama shows.

One Sunday morning, we used the small computer to get on Facebook Live for church. Robert logged in from his page and didn't log out when the service was over.

Down in the DM

The next day, Robert left to take his mom to the grocery store. I started washing clothes and decided to get on the computer. I logged onto the Walmart website to see if they had any Lysol spray in stock. Then, I went to the Amazon website to check out their daily specials. Not finding anything, I clicked the Facebook icon and it opened, still logged into Robert's account. He had a couple of messages. Yes, I clicked on the notifications to see who had sent him direct messages. It was a couple of Christian messages from a couple of family members, some disrespectful meme messages from one of his coworkers, with a nude woman's pictures attached, and a message from a young lady who he seemed to be constantly communicating with.

I read through the messages. They talked about her kids and her job, and she asked him about his mother. Then, he asked her what she'd cooked for dinner and what kind of dishes she could cook. By this time, I was livid. My heart was beating a mile a minute. After looking at her profile, I found out that this young lady was in her twenties. *What in the hell is on his mind?* I asked myself. I scrolled all the way to the beginning of the first message, which showed me that he had been conversing with this young lady for over a week. They also talked about taking a test because Robert didn't know, and he wanted to be sure. Suddenly, it all made sense. That was why he had been spending so much time in the basement on Facebook and on his phone. He'd been talking to *her*.

I closed the page and called him, trying to remain calm. I was gonna let him have it when he walked through that door if he pulled up before I called him. I went to the living room to see if his car was outside and it wasn't. I called him on his cell phone.

"Hey, where you at?" I asked.

"I just dropped Mama off and I'm on my way back home. What's up?"

"Oh, okay. Well, we have to talk when you get here."

"What's wrong? Is it good or bad?"

"I will let you be the judge of that."

"Okay," he said. "I will be there in about ten minutes."

I was walking back and forth from the living room to the bedroom, pissed off. As soon as he came through the door, I couldn't hold it any longer.

"Who is this chick in your inbox? I guess the saying is true about how it goes down in the DM because you been down and in, huh?"

He was quiet. He held his head down.

"Bae, I was gonna tell you about her," he said. "I just didn't know how you were going to feel because I don't know for sure myself."

"You don't know what?"

"She said I'm her father!"

My mouth dropped. "What?"

"Yeah. All these years, I never knew. She said her mom said I was her father."

"Did you ever have a relationship with her mother?"

"No! We were just booty buddies! I didn't know how you would feel, or if this would affect our marriage."

"I'm your wife! You should be able to tell me anything."

He assured me that he was going to tell me. He just needed to try to grasp it himself and think about if it could be true.

"This is just as shocking to me as it is to you. But she's a grown woman. She was there before we got married if the test proves she is your daughter. Now, had something like this happened while we were married, of course we would have a different outcome."

"I want to get a blood test done to find out the truth. If she is mine, I would like to welcome her into our family."

I agreed. He has spoken to her and they agreed to set some time to get the test done based on COVID-19 and their work schedules. We sat down and revisited not only our vows, but everything that happened from the first day I got sick up until the day we had a heart-to-heart talk on how to have bumps and stomps in marriage, but keep it moving.

Being in a pandemic with my husband showed us not only our strengths, but our weaknesses, our faults and our feelings. It showed us how situations can cause you to grow closer together or further apart. We just celebrated five years of marriage on April 18, 2020, and we are striving for forever. We have never been in a pandemic, but we both have been in previous marriages that ended in divorce.

We strive hard to preserve our marriage on a daily basis, even when it seems overwhelming. Life can throw a lot of curveballs at you. In a marriage, you must have a team player who is willing to help you catch some of those curveballs. Or else you get hit and will be down and out for the count. I'm glad that I have a team player on my team, and we work well together. I created *Fun and Marriage* to help couples get through happy times and bad times. All marriages may not end in "happily ever after." But for those couples who want to intentionally preserve their marriage, we help them do so through games, tools and materials that help build a sustainable marriage.

Marriage Uncut
CHECKPOINT

1. Do you think the parents handled the situation with their son leaving the house in a pandemic the first time appropriately?

2. Being a blended family, could this pandemic have caused major problems in this story?

3. Should the wife have closed her husband's Facebook page and not checked his inbox messages if she didn't have his permission?

4. Was the husband wrong for not telling his wife about the young lady possibly being his daughter when he first found out, or did he do the right thing by waiting to tell his wife?

5. How can revisiting your vows from time to time keep your marriage intact?

About the Author
➤ Ortavia McClain

Marriage is hard work, and you must be a team player. The job can be overwhelming at times, especially when you have a blended family. Even though it may be hard, and take some time getting used to, it can be done. With God in the center, love on top, communication, commitment, and trust by your side, you can build a sustainable marriage. In Ortavia McClain's first marriage, there was no building. Of course, the marriage fell apart. She realized that some losses could lead her right into destiny. The pain and hurt she went through in her first marriage prepared her for her second marriage. She believes God is a vital part in marriage, and that He's the Creator and the tie that binds. Today, she is the founder and CEO of Fun and Marriage. Fun and Marriage host events for traditionally married couples and creates strategic interactive games, fun events and educational materials that help build and restore marriages.

For more information on bookings and events, email funandmarriage@gmail.com and visit www.funandmarriage.com.

Brown Sugar
by Tenita C. Johnson

When COVID-19 hit the U.S., me and Jermaine, my husband of seventeen years, were just returning from an all-expense paid trip to Las Vegas. One of the perks of being a manager at his job was the fact that he had to speak at conferences annually in Las Vegas, a destination we were always excited to visit. We'd spent the week enjoying the sights, food and fun in what many people call "Sin City." However, it was more than a blessing to us.

We flew back to Detroit Sunday, March 1, 2020.

By Thursday, March 5, our schools had shut down for what we thought was an extended weekend to simply disinfect the schools. Little did we know that it would be the last time our children would step inside their school buildings for months. By the following Monday, we'd received notice that we had to come to the schools to pick up work for the next two weeks, with expectation the schools would reopen by the latter part of the month, at the latest. One week turned into two. Two weeks turned into two months. Two months turned into what seemed to me as a six-month long summer vacation.

Suddenly, I was thrust into a homeschool position I'd never applied for—nor did I want. As a full-time entrepreneur, I don't work forty-hour work weeks. I work twelve- or sixteen-hour days most days, with little to no time to cook, throw a load of laundry in or pick up my daughter from the carpool point. So, I surely didn't have time to teach both a sophomore and a second grader, both of which seem to work my patience to no end.

At first, my husband still worked full-time in the office. So, I was at home with the children daily for weeks. Even though school started for both of them long before 8 a.m. under normal circumstances, most days, I opted for letting them sleep in until noon so I could get a great chunk of work done in my business before I had to switch hats to teacher mode. My husband didn't think that was a great idea. He often told my son to get up at 7 a.m., just like he was going to school, to complete his work for the day. But then, my husband would be out the door, heading to work. I was left here, answering questions and putting out fires and fights among these young people who thought they were on vacation long term.

However, eventually, my husband started working from home. He was able to see firsthand the challenges I was having as a business owner, homemaker, cook, maid, mama and teacher.

I felt like I was failing tremendously at them all at one time. Even though we read the Word of God every morning before my husband rushed out the door, as soon as he left, it was as if that peace of God that we'd read about had disappeared into thin air. When he started working from home, we read the Word in the morning and he would retreat to the basement, where his home office is set up.

Suddenly, the tone of the whole house changed.

My son and daughter seemed to listen to him *the first time* he told them to do something. Meanwhile, I had to threaten them with a belt to get them to do even remotely what I'd asked them to do four or five times. He often cooked breakfast for the family when he didn't have to be on a conference call early in the morning. When he didn't make breakfast, he made sure he'd come upstairs for lunchtime to spend a few moments with the family. While I worked diligently in my office, oftentimes flipping between Zoom calls and phone conferences, he would sneak in and drop a plate of shrimp and fries, or chicken, or a grilled cheese on my desk and whisper, "Babe, I brought you lunch."

When he noticed my frustration with my daughter's frustration about her online learning exercises daily, he would come upstairs and work with her for an hour to get it complete in record time. He made sure that the children not only cleaned their rooms daily, but that they did their household chores that they often fought me tooth and nail about when I even mentioned the chore list.

We spent many mornings listening to worship online on YouTube or Apple Music, setting the atmosphere of the home to a state of calm when all I could see was chaos because there was so much to do. Yet, there seemed to be so little time in a day to get things done. With churches state-wide being shut down due to the pandemic as well, we started a new tradition: breakfast and worship on Sunday mornings before tuning into our local church online service. By the time we arrived at our service online, we were already charged up and ready to hear the Word. We didn't just watch our local church online, though.

We indulged in many popular ministries and took advantage of the fact that we could travel to North Carolina, then to Atlanta, followed by Rochester, Michigan, then back to Atlanta—all in a matter of four hours. We listened to Pastor Steven Furtick, Pastor John Gray, Pastor Corey Williams of Impact Church in Savannah, Georgia, followed by our very own pastor, Dominic Russo of Oakland Church. By 1 p.m., we were both ready for our "after church nap" many Sundays. One thing was for sure: In the midst of a pandemic, our spiritual intimacy was heightened.

In addition, we spent many days and nights reminiscing by listening to 90s R&B and indulging in old school hip-hop. We listened to everything from Shai and Jodeci, to Mary J. Blige, Jagged Edge and Babyface. But then, we took a step back further into time. We found ourselves falling asleep to hits from Luther Vandross, Stevie Wonder, TLC, Brandy and Brian McKnight. There's something about *music*. It has the power to transform rooms and moods. When we didn't fall asleep to the sounds of rain or thunderstorms on the Calm app, we spent many nights searching Apple Music for the "oldies but goodies" we listened to in those days when we first met.

Long story short, we met when I was fourteen years old. He was eighteen. We'd managed to keep in contact over the course of ten years via letters, phone calls and email since he was in the United States Marine Corps from 1994 to 2000. And even in the midst of him traveling overseas, fighting in wars, and landing in North Carolina for his long-term service assignment, we never lost touch. Whenever we thought we were "done," he knew how to reach me. He knew who to call and he knew how to find me when he came home to Detroit. Even though I'd left Detroit, went to college in Missouri for four years, worked at Walt Disney

World in Florida for six months, and moved back to Missouri—all in the course of five years—I knew how to find *him*. No matter who we dated or slept with, no matter who we tried to have a relationship with, there was no one like the other.

Something, somewhere, always drew us right back to where we started: *each other.*

If you've read Marriage Uncut: Straight Talk, No Chaser or Marriage Uncut II: Straight Talk, No Chaser, you know we've overcome our fair share of storms. Infidelity and adultery. Death of children. Unemployment. Debt. Garnishment. Miscarriages. Blended family woes. Separation. Mental illness. Depression and suicidal thoughts. Physical abuse (from me abusing him, not the other way around). You name it, we more than likely have conquered it.

But a *pandemic*? We had not yet been through one of those, let alone conquered it. Suddenly, the usual hustle and bustle of everyday life stopped, and we were all put on mandatory time-out. I got plenty of calls from wives who were irritated, frustrated and ready to get a divorce because they suddenly had to be in the house every day, all day, with a spouse they didn't halfway like *before* COVID hit—let alone now. Since we have overcome much in our seventeen years of marriage, many couples reach out to us for wise counsel and coaching. And the calls from both wives and husbands increased overnight.

However, the opposite happened for us, to us. We leaned into each other. We leaned on each other more. We had deeper conversations. We asked deeper questions. We prayed deeper prayers. We saw the Word of God in a new light and, every time we read Bible verses, they seemed to leap off the page as awe-inspiring moments. We dreamed a bit deeper. We filed LLC paperwork for several new businesses. We invested. We sowed. We gave. We poured into others. And as we poured, more was poured into us. We, in an instant, learned to redefine *love*. We learned to redefine the definition of the *Church*. We learned to love without boundaries. We learned to listen to hear more, not simply to respond. We learned to speak from the heart and listen to the heart behind the words—even those unspoken. It was a divine reset for our marriage, and we've been abundantly blessed because of the pandemic interrupting our regularly scheduled program to catapult us to a new normal.

It's not ideal. Going through a pandemic is uncomfortable and unconventional. It's scary, and it's lifechanging. But one thing remains a constant in our marriage: The power of music always transports us back to the core of love created the first time we first kissed. The first time we made love. The first time we shared a hotel together on a beach in North Carolina.

Just like in the movie *Brown Sugar*, I always have to ask myself, "When did you fall in love with hip-hop?"

He is the beat of my heart. The yin to my yang. My covering. My friend. My confidant. He's been my life partner and my lifeline when I thought life was over. The very air that I breathe and the gateway to happiness and joy. It all started when I met him at the tender age of fourteen years old and I could only dream of having a husband and a family of my own.

When did I fall in love with hip-hop?

Hip-hop is *he*.

He is my hip-hop.

And I fell in love with him—*again*—in the spring of 2020, in the midst of a worldwide pandemic. He's my *brown sugar*.

Marriage Uncut
CHECKPOINT

1. How do you redefine love post-pandemic?
   _____
   _____

2. What, or who, has been your "hip-hop" in life?
   _____
   _____

3. How has the pandemic changed your viewpoint of love, marriage and relationships?
   _____
   _____

4. What does spiritual intimacy mean to you?
   _____
   _____

5. How do you define emotional and mental intimacy in a marriage?
   _____
   _____

About the Author
➥ Tenita C. Johnson

From losing a set of twins the day after she and her husband were married, to years of unemployment, suicidal thoughts and blended family woes, she soon learned that the only way out of every fire is to go *through* it. After going through the fire numerous times, and coming out unscathed, she realized that every fire was orchestrated by God to burn some things off of her to make her better. Not only that, every fire gave her a greater testimony to share with others who may be encountering the same things.

Through her books, Tenita encourages readers nationwide to know that with every test comes a predetermined victory. The young girl who once thought she wasn't good enough has blossomed into a woman of faith who knows that, with God, she is more than just enough. She makes a deliberate choice to live her best life now and walk in her God-given purpose daily and encourages others to do the same.

For more information, visit www.soitiswritten.net.

About
So It Is Written, LLC

We are a full-service content writing and editorial company, designed to assist with your every need as it relates to the written word. Writing and editing can be extremely time consuming. The words in your book are crucial to your overall success. They can make or break you. But we can help!

So It Is Written, LLC believes in the quality of the written word and drafting content in excellence. Whether it's editing manuscripts for bestselling authors or ghostwriting for the author who just doesn't have the time to complete his/her manuscript, we have what it takes to fulfill your literary needs.

Call us at 313-999-6942 today or email info@soitiswritten.net for more details about our personalized writing and editing services. We look forward to working with you to make your project one of excellence!

About
The Red Ink Conference

Known as the Premier Conference for authors, editors, playwrights and more, this writing conference empowers attendees from around the nation to write, edit and market their next bestseller in excellence. Many of the attendees are indie authors who are just starting their publishing journey. We're inviting aspiring bestsellers, as well as those who want to take their writing to the next level by editing for other indie authors, to join us in this year in one of two locations–or both! Our expert presenters have over 20 years of industry experience and run successful businesses that support indie authors nationwide. We're excited to make a dent in the book publishing world and have our attendees learn new, innovative information that will position them to build a solid platform as an author and speaker. For more information, visit theredinkconference.com.

www.ingramcontent.com/pod-product-compliance
Lightning Source LLC
Chambersburg PA
CBHW071851070526
44583CB00016B/1646